THE GIFT
OF DEATH
&
LITERATURE
IN SECRET

THE GIFT
OF DEATH

SECOND EDITION

&

LITERATURE
IN SECRET

JACQUES DERRIDA

TRANSLATED BY
DAVID WILLS

THE UNIVERSITY OF CHICAGO PRESS
CHICAGO AND LONDON

Originally published as *Donner la mort* by Jacques Derrida, copyright
© Éditions Galilée 1999.

The University of Chicago Press, Chicago 60637
The University of Chicago Press, Ltd., London
© 1995, 2008 by The University of Chicago
All rights reserved. Published 2008
Paperback edition 2017
Printed in the United States of America

32 31 30 29 28 27 26 25 24 23   1 2 3 4 5

ISBN-13: 978-0-226-50297-7 (paper)
ISBN-13: 978-0-226-57167-6 (e-book)

Library of Congress Cataloging-in-Publication Data
Derrida, Jacques.
        [Donner la mort. English]
        The gift of death ; and, Literature in secret / Jacques Derrida ;
Translated by David Wills.—2nd ed.
        p.   cm.
Includes bibliographical references.
ISBN-13: 978-0-226-14276-0 (cloth. : alk. paper)
ISBN-13: 978-0-226-14277-7 (pbk. : alk. paper)
ISBN-10: 0-226-14276-0 (cloth. : alk. paper)
ISBN-10: 0-226-14277-9 (pbk. : alk. paper)
        1. Generosity. 2. Gifts. 3. Responsibility.   I. Derrida, Jacques.
Literature in secret.   II. Title.   III. Title: Literature in secret.
        B2430.D483D6613 2008
        194—dc22

                                                                    2007024288

∞ The paper used in this publication meets the minimum requirements
of the American National Standard for Information Sciences—Perma-
nence of Paper for Printed Library Materials, ANSI Z39.48-1992.

CONTENTS

TRANSLATOR'S PREFACE
TO THE 2007 EDITION

The Gift of Death was originally translated from the essay Derrida published in a collection of papers from a conference held at Royaumont in December 1990 on "The Ethics of the Gift" (ed. Jean-Michel Rabaté and Michael Wetzel, *L'Éthique du don: Jacques Derrida et la pensée du don, Colloque de Royaumont, 1990* [Paris: Transition, 1992]). Derrida's text was not, however, the paper he delivered at that conference, that being part of a volume already destined for publication (*Donner le temps* [Paris: Galilée, 1991]) and now translated as *Given Time: 1. Counterfeit Money*, trans. Peggy Kamuf (Chicago: University of Chicago Press, 1992).

In 1999, he published the volume *Donner la mort* (Paris: Galilée), containing the original text as well as an essay on Kafka entitled "La littérature au secret." The present edition represents the first complete English translation of that volume, including a thorough revision of the 1995 English publication of *The Gift of Death* (Chicago: University of Chicago) on the basis of both Derrida's emendations of his own text and my corrections of my earlier version, as well as the addition of the first English translation of the Kafka essay.

The French title *Donner la mort* plays on the ordinary sense of *donner*, meaning "to give," and the idiomatic sense of that expression, which means in English "to put to death," as in *se donner la mort*, "to commit suicide." In translating Derrida's title with the noun phrase I seek to have heard in it (or behind it) the English expression "kiss of death," as a means of conveying that "active" sense. Wherever possible I have tried to follow the idea of "giving" or "granting," having recourse to "to put to death" when comprehensibility so demands, sometimes adding the French for mnemonic purposes. Whenever "to put to death" is used, however, the reader should also hear the sense of "giving."

The 1999 Galilée edition of *Donner la mort* was accompanied by the following text in the form of a flysheet (*Prière d'insérer*):

In spite of various indications, in spite of the sign of the gift, in spite of the predictable passage from time to death, in spite of the albeit furtive appearance of the narrator of Baudelaire's "Counterfeit Money," *Donner la mort* is not a sequel to *Given Time: 1. Counterfeit Money*.

The consistently *dominant* figure here is Abraham: certainly he who, above all, received the three men who were God's envoys at the Oak of Mambre, and *gave* them hospitality, thereby inaugurating a whole tradition. But this Abraham is also he who, after all, *knows how he must keep silent* [*sait devoir se taire*] on Mount Moriah, up until the angel, another envoy from God, interrupts the death that he is preparing—in order to *give* it to God—to *impose* [*donner*] on his favorite son Isaac; unless it be, as in the lands of Islam, Ibrahim's Ishmael.

How does one interpret Abraham's secret and the law requiring his silence? Why does it seem incommensurable with the interdiction that seems to reduce all his family to a type of muteness: all those, male and female, to whom he has, all the same, never confided anything; as well as Sarah and Isaac, Hagar and Ishmael, who were so summarily dismissed? It is those four who were closest to him, made to play the part of extras, whom we intend to bring discreetly back to center stage.

One no longer knows how to understand the indecipherability of this unheard-of moment. One no longer knows how to reinterpret it. One no longer knows, because it is no longer a question of knowledge, who has the prerogative to reinterpret the infinite number of interpretations that have always foundered here in view of the shore, or sunk into the abyssal depths that open for our memory, being discovered and covering over themselves at the same time.

Yet we are that memory, forewarned and summoned by it. Our reason forces us to take it on board on the high seas and just prior to our shipwreck [*arraisonnés en pleine mer et avant le naufrage*]. It assigns to us an inalienable heritage. Granted, we can deny it, but all the same it remains undeniable, and continues to dictate to us a certain reading of the world. A reading of what a "world" means. Indeed, a reading of the contemporary globalization of avowal, repentance, and forgiveness. According to Kierkegaard's writings, Abraham asked for God's forgiveness, not for having betrayed him, but for having obeyed him!

The history of Europe, of responsibility, of subjectivity, and of secrecy, the possibility of literature, perhaps those are some of the names, among others, perhaps the nicknames, of what is at stake here.

In addition, the more than One. And the question of knowing why, by means of its Abrahamic filiation, literature would be required to ask forgiveness—for not meaning (to say) [*de ne pas vouloir dire*]. And why God would still have to swear.

We will pay heed here to several great vigil-keepers, brought together around the biblical corpus. All of them are men. They argue over the night. Kierkegaard first of all, Kierkegaard indefinitely, and Kafka especially, and Melville, but also Patočka, following after Plato, Nietzsche, Heidegger, and Lévinas.

THE GIFT
OF DEATH

JACQUES DERRIDA

TRANSLATED BY
DAVID WILLS

ONE

Secrets of European Responsibility

In one of his *Heretical Essays on the Philosophy of History*[1] Jan Patočka relates secrecy,[2] or more precisely the mystery of the sacred, to responsibility. He opposes one to the other; or rather underscores their heterogeneity. Somewhat in the manner of Lévinas he warns against an experience of the sacred as an enthusiasm or fervor for fusion, cautioning in particular against a form of demonic rapture that has as its effect, and often as its first intention, the removal of responsibility, the loss of the sense or consciousness[3] of responsibility. At the same time Patočka wants to distinguish religion from

1. "Is Technological Civilization Decadent, and Why?" in Jan Patočka, *Heretical Essays in the Philosophy of History*, trans. Erazim Kohák, ed. James Dodd (Chicago: Open Court, 1996). Page references to this edition will henceforth appear in parentheses following the citation. Where the original Czech is provided it has been added by Derrida.

2. In French *le secret* refers both to "a secret" and to the more abstract sense of "secrecy." In general I have used whichever alternative better suits the syntax.—Trans.

3. French *conscience* translates as both "conscience" and "consciousness." I have used either, according to the syntax, often preferring "conscience" rather than to presume to distinguish among the physiological, psychological, or moral senses of the French word, especially because Derrida's analysis of responsibility calls those distinctions into question.—Trans.

the demonic form of sacralization. What is a religion? Religion presumes access to the responsibility of a free self. It thus implies breaking with this type of secrecy (for it is not of course the only one), that associated with sacred mystery and with what Patočka regularly calls the demonic. A distinction is to be made between the demonic on the one hand (that which confuses the limits among the animal, the human, and the divine, and which retains an affinity with mystery, the initiatory, the esoteric, the secret or the sacred) and responsibility on the other. This therefore amounts to a thesis on the origin and essence of the religious.

Under what conditions can one speak of a religion, in the proper sense of the term, presuming such a sense exists? Under what conditions can we speak of a history of religion, and first and foremost of the Christian religion? In noting that Patočka refers only to the example of his own religion I do not seek to denounce an omission or establish the guilt of a failure to develop a comparative analysis. On the contrary, it seems necessary to reinforce the coherence of a way of thinking that takes into account the event of Christian mystery as an absolute singularity, a religion par excellence and an irreducible condition for a joint history of the subject, responsibility, and Europe. That is so even if, here and there, the expression "history of religion*s*" appears in the plural, and even if, also, one can infer from this plural a reference to Judaic, Islamic, and Christian religions alone, those known as religions of the Book.[4]

According to Patočka, one can only speak of religion once the demonic secret, and the orgiastic sacred, have been *surpassed*. We should let that term retain its essential ambiguity. In the proper sense of the word, religion exists once the secret of the sacred, orgiastic, or demonic mystery has been, if not destroyed, at least integrated, and finally subjected to the sphere of responsibility. The subject of responsibility will be the subject that has managed to make orgiastic or demonic mystery subject to itself. But it has done

4. I refer there to a set of questions that are approached, from another point of view, in my "Faith and Knowledge: The Two Sources of 'Religion' at the Limits of Reason Alone," trans. Samuel Weber, in *Religion*, ed. Jacques Derrida and Gianni Vattimo (Stanford: Stanford University Press, 1998).

that only in order, at the same time, to freely subject itself to the wholly and infinite other that sees without being seen. Religion is responsibility or it is nothing at all. Its history derives its sense entirely from the idea of a *passage* to responsibility. Such a passage involves traversing or enduring the test by means of which the ethical conscience will be delivered of the demonic, the mystagogic, and the enthusiastic, of the initiatory and the esoteric. In the authentic sense of the word, religion comes into being the moment that the experience of responsibility extracts itself from that form of secrecy called demonic mystery.

Since the concept of the *daimon* crosses the boundaries separating the human from the animal and the divine, it comes as no surprise to see Patočka recognize in it an essential dimension of sexual desire. In what respect does this demonic mystery of desire involve us in a history of responsibility, more precisely in history *as* responsibility?

"The demonic needs to be brought into a relation with responsibility as originally and primarily it is not" (100). In other words, the demonic is originally defined as irresponsibility, or, if one wishes, as nonresponsibility. It belongs to a space that does not yet resound with the injunction to *respond*, a space in which one does not yet hear the call to explain oneself [*répondre de soi*], one's actions, or one's thoughts, to respond to the other and answer for oneself before the other. The genesis of responsibility that Patočka proposes will not simply describe a history of religion or religiousness. It will overlap with a genealogy of the subject who says "myself," the subject's relation to itself as an instance of liberty, singularity, and responsibility, the relation to self as being before the other: the other in its infinite alterity, one who regards without being seen but also whose infinite goodness *gives* in an experience that amounts to a *gift of death* [*donner la mort*]. For the moment let us leave that expression in all its ambiguity.

Of course, since this genealogy is also a history of sexuality, it follows the traces of a genius of Christianity that is the history of Europe. For at the center of Patočka's essay the stakes are clearly defined as follows: how to interpret "the *birth* of Europe in the present sense of the word" (109)? How to conceive of "European expansion" (110) before and after the Crusades? More radically still, what is it that ails "modern civilization" inasmuch as it is European? Not that it suffers from a particular fault or from a particular form of blindness. Simply, why does it suffer from ignorance of its history, from a failure to assume its responsibility, that is, the memory of its history *as* history of responsibility?

This misunderstanding does not betray an accidental failing on the part of the scholar or philosopher. It is not in fact a sin of ignorance or lack of knowledge. It is not because they *don't know* [*faute de savoir*] that Europeans do not read their history as a history of responsibility. European historians' misunderstanding of historicity, which is in the first place a misunderstanding of what links historicity to responsibility, is explained on the contrary by the extent to which their historical knowledge occludes, precludes, or saturates those questions, grounds, or abysses, naively presuming to totalize or naturalize them, or, what amounts to the same thing, losing themselves in the details. For at the heart of this history there is something of an abyss [*il y a de l'abîme*], an abyss that resists totalizing summary. Separating orgiastic mystery from Christian mystery, this abyss also announces the origin of responsibility. Such is the conclusion that the whole essay moves toward:

> Modern civilization suffers not only from its own flaws and myopia but also from the failure to resolve the entire problem of history. Yet the problem of history may not be resolved; it must be preserved as a problem. Today the danger is that knowing so many particulars, we are losing the ability to see the questions and that which is their foundation.
>
> Perhaps the entire question about the decadence of civilization is incorrectly posed. There is no civilization as such. The question is whether historical humans are still willing to embrace history (*přiznávat se k dějinám*). (118)

This last sentence suggests that historicity remains a secret. Historical humans do not want to *admit to* historicity, and first and foremost to the abyss that undermines their own historicity. Why should one admit to history? And why would such a confession be difficult?

Two reasons might be given for this resistance to such an admission.

On the one hand, the history of responsibility is tied to a history of religion. But there is always a risk in acknowledging a *history* of responsibility. It is often thought, on the basis of an analysis of the very concepts of responsibility, freedom, or decision, that to be responsible, free, or capable of deciding cannot be something that is acquired, something conditioned or conditional. Even if there is undeniably a history of freedom or responsibility, such a historicity, it is thought, must remain *extrinsic*. It must not interfere with the essence of an experience that consists precisely in tearing oneself away from one's own historical conditions. What would responsibility be if it were motivated, conditioned, made possible by a history? Although some might think that there is no exercise of responsibility except in a manner that is essentially historical, the classic concept of decision and responsibility seems to exclude from the essence, heart, or proper moment of responsible *decision* all historical connections (whether they be genealogical or not, whether their causality be mechanical or dialectical, or even if they derive from other types of motivation or programming such as those that relate to a psychoanalytic history). It is therefore difficult to *admit to* such a historicity and, inasmuch as a whole ethics of responsibility often claims to separate itself, as ethics, from religious revelation, it is even more difficult to bind it, in its essence, to a history of religion.

On the other hand, if Patočka says that this historicity must be *admitted to*, implying thereby that it is something difficult to acknowledge, that is because historicity must *remain open* as a problem, never to be resolved: "the problem of history . . . must be preserved as a problem" (118). The moment the problem were resolved that very totalizing closure would determine the end of history: it would bring in the verdict of nonhistoricity itself. History can be neither a decidable object nor a totality capable of being mastered, precisely because it is tied to *responsibility*, to *faith* and to the *gift*. To *responsibility* in the experience of absolute decisions that involve breaking with knowledge or given norms, made therefore through the very ordeal of the undecidable; to religious *faith* through a form

7

of involvement with or relation to the other that is a venture into absolute risk, beyond knowledge and certainty; to the *gift* and to the gift of death that puts me into relation with the transcendence of the other—with God as selfless goodness—and that gives me what it gives me through a new experience of death. Responsibility and faith go together, however paradoxical that might seem to some, and both should, in the same movement, exceed mastery and knowledge. The gift of death would be this marriage of responsibility and faith. History depends on such an excessive beginning [*ouverture*].

The paradox here plays on *two heterogeneous types of secret*: on the one hand the secret of historicity, what historical man has difficulty acknowledging but which he *must* admit to because it concerns his very responsibility; and on the other hand the secret of orgiastic mystery that the history of responsibility has to break with.

An additional complication further overdetermines the breadth or abyss of this experience. Why speak of secrecy where Patočka states that it is historicity that must be acknowledged? This becoming-responsible, that is, this becoming-historical of humankind, seems to be intimately tied to the properly Christian event of *another secret*, or more precisely of a mystery, the *mysterium tremendum*: the terrifying mystery, the dread, fear, and trembling of the Christian in the experience of the sacrificial gift. This trembling seizes one at the moment of becoming a person, and the person can only become what it is in being paralyzed [*transie*], in its very singularity, by the gaze of God. Then the person sees itself seen by the gaze of another, "the absolute highest being in whose hands we are, not externally, but internally" (106).

This passage from exteriority to interiority, but also from the accessible to the inaccessible, assures the transition from Platonism to Christianity. It is held that, starting from a responsibility and ethico-political self of the Platonic type, there occurs a mutation that liberates the responsibility of the Christian self, although such a self remains to be thought through. For this is indeed one of Patočka's *Heretical Essays*: it doesn't fail to note in passing that Christianity has perhaps not yet thought through the very essence of the self whose arrival it nevertheless records. Christianity has not yet accorded such a self the thematic value it deserves: "What a Person is, that really is not adequately thematized in the Christian perspective" (107).

The secret of the *mysterium tremendum* takes over from a heterogeneous secrecy and at the same time breaks with it. This rupture takes the form of either subordination by *incorporation* (one secret subjects or silences the other), or *repression*. The mysterium tremendum *gets carried away* [*s'emporte*] in the double sense of the term: it rises *against* another mystery but it rises *on the back* [*sur le fond*] *of* a past mystery. At base [*au fond*] it represses, repressing what remains its basis [*son fond*]. The secret that the event of Christianity takes to task is at the same time a form of Platonism—or Neoplatonism—which retains something of the thaumaturgical tradition, and the secret of orgiastic mystery from which Plato had already tried to deliver philosophy. Hence the history of responsibility is particularly multilayered. The history of the responsible self is built upon the heritage and *patrimony* of secrecy, through a chain reaction of ruptures and repressions that assure the very tradition they punctuate with their interruptions. Plato breaks with orgiastic mystery and installs a first experience based on the notion of responsibility, but there remains something of demonic mystery and thaumaturgy, as well as some of responsibility's corresponding political dimension, in Platonism as in Neoplatonism. Then comes the *mysterium tremendum* of Christian responsibility, second tremor in the genesis of responsibility as a history of secrecy, but also, as we shall see a little later, a tremor in the figures of death as figures of the gift, or in fact as gifts of death [*de la mort donnée*].

This history will never come to a close. Any history worthy of the name can never be saturated or sutured. This history of secrecy that humans, in particular Christians, have difficulty thematizing, even more so acknowledging, is punctuated by many reversals, or more precisely conversions. Patočka uses the word "conversion" as one often does to render the ascending movement of *anabasis* by which Plato calls for turning one's gaze toward the Good and the intelligible sun, out of the cavern (a Good that is not yet goodness and so remains foreign to the idea of the gift). The word "conversion" is regularly rendered by words such as "reversal" (*obrácení*,

104) or "about-face" (*obrat*, 106). The history of secrecy, the combined history of responsibility and of the gift, has the spiral form of these turns, intricacies, versions, turnings back, bends, and conversions. One could compare it to a history of revolutions, even to history as revolution.

Taking Eugen Fink as his authority, Patočka describes the very space of Platonic speleology as the subterranean basis of orgiastic mysteries. The cavern becomes the Earth Mother from which one must finally extract oneself in order to "subordinate," as Patočka puts it, "the *orgiastic* entirely to responsibility" (*podřídit orgiasmus zodpovědnosti*, 104). But Platonic *anabasis* does not provide a passage from orgiastic mystery to nonmystery. It is the subordination of one mystery by another, the conversion from one secret to another. For Patočka calls the Platonic conversion that turns an eternal gaze toward the Good a "new *mystery* of the soul." This time the mystery becomes more internal, it takes the form of "the soul's interior dialogue" (105). Although it does correspond to a first awakening of responsibility by means of the soul's relation to the Good, this coming-to-conscience does not yet separate from its mystical element; it still takes the form of a mystery, this time unacknowledged, undeclared, denied.

One can already recognize the law for which this serves as a first example. Like those which will follow Plato's *anabasis* throughout a history of responsibility that capitalizes on secrecy, this first conversion still retains within it something of what it seems to interrupt. The logic of this conservative rupture resembles the *economy of a sacrifice* that keeps what it gives up. Sometimes it reminds one of the economy of sublation [*relève*] or *Aufhebung*, and at other times, less contradictory than it seems, of a logic of repression that still retains what is denied, surpassed, buried. Repression doesn't destroy, it displaces from one place to another within the system. It is also a topological operation. In fact Patočka often has recourse to a type of psychoanalytic vocabulary. In the double conversion that he analyzes (that which turns away from orgiastic mystery toward Platonic or Neoplatonic mystery, as well as that which converts the latter into the Christian *mysterium tremendum*), it is true that the earlier mystery is "subordinated" (*podřazeno*) by that which follows, but it is never eliminated. In order to better describe this hierarchical subordination Patočka speaks of "incorporation" or "repression": incorporation (*přivtělení*) in the case of Platonism, which retains within itself the orgiastic mystery it subordinates, subjects and disciplines, but *repression* (*potlačeni*) in the case of Christianity, which suppresses yet retains Platonic mystery.

As a result, everything happens as though conversion amounted to a process of mourning, facing up to a loss, in the sense of keeping within oneself that whose death one must endure. And what one keeps inside at the very moment that there comes into play a new experience of secrecy and a new structure of responsibility as apportioning of mystery, is the buried memory or crypt of a more ancient secret.

To what extent should I be permitted to take literally the words *incorporation* and *repression*, which I come across in the French translation of Patočka? Did he wish to give them the conceptual contours that they possess within psychoanalytic discourse, notably in a theory of mourning? Even if that is not the case, nothing prevents us from putting a psychoanalytic reading of these words to the test, at least on an experimental basis; or if not a psychoanalytic reading, at least a hermeneutics that takes into account the psychoanalytic concepts corresponding to the words "incorporation" and "repression," especially since our problematic comes to a point around the motif of secrecy. Such a motif cannot remain immune to notions of *incorporation* (especially with respect to the work of mourning and to the figures of death that are necessarily associated with absolute secrecy) and *repression*, as the privileged process of every effect of secrecy. Historical conversions to responsibility, such as Patočka analyzes in both cases, well describe this movement by which the event of a second mystery fails to destroy the first. On the contrary it keeps it inside unconsciously after having effected a topical displacement and a hierarchical subordination: one secret is at the same time enclosed and dominated by the other. Platonic mystery thus *incorporates* orgiastic mystery, and Christian mystery *represses* Platonic mystery. That, in short, is the history that would need to be "admitted to," as if confessed! In order to avoid speaking of secrecy where Patočka speaks of mystery one would be tempted to say that secrecy—what must be acknowledged and analyzed as historicity itself—is here the secret relation between these two conversions and these three mysteries (orgiastic, Platonic, and Christian). The history to be acknowledged is the secret of incorporation and repression, what occurs between one conversion and another. It concerns the time of conversion, and what is at stake in it, namely the gift of death.

For this is not just one theme among others: a history of secrecy as history of responsibility is tied to a culture of death, in other words, to the different figures of the gift of death or of putting to death [*la mort donnée*].[5] What does the French expression *donner la mort* mean? How does one give *oneself* death [se *donner la mort*]? How does one give it to oneself in the sense that putting oneself to death means dying while assuming responsibility for one's own death, committing suicide but also sacrificing oneself for another, *dying for the other*, thus perhaps giving one's life by giving oneself death, accepting the gift of death, such as Socrates, Christ, and others did in so many different ways. And perhaps Patočka in his own way? How does one give oneself death in that other sense where *se donner la mort* also means to interpret death, to give oneself a representation of it, a figure, a signification or destination for it? How does one give it to oneself in the sense of simply, and more generally, relating to the possibility of death (on the basis of what care for, or apprehension of, it?) even if that means, following Heidegger, relating to the possibility of an impossibility? What is the relation between *se donner la mort* and sacrifice? Between putting oneself to death and dying for another? What are the relations among sacrifice, suicide, and the economy of this gift?

The incorporation by means of which Platonic responsibility triumphs over orgiastic mystery is the movement by which the immortality of the individual soul is affirmed—it is also the death given to Socrates, the death that he is given and that he accepts, in

5. Literature concerning the secret is almost always organized around scenes and intrigues that deal with figures of death. This is something I attempt to demonstrate elsewhere, referring most often to "American" examples ("The Purloined Letter," "Bartleby the Scrivener," "The Figure in the Carpet," *The Aspern Papers*, etc.) that are the subjects of a recent seminar on the conjoined questions of secrecy and responsibility.

other words the death that he in a way gives himself when in the *Phaedo* he develops a whole discourse to give sense to his death and as it were to take the responsibility for it upon himself.

Concerning the allegory of the cave, and following Fink, Patočka writes,

> This presentation, especially its dramatic part, is a *reversal* (*obrácení*) of the traditional mysteries and of their orgiastic cults. Those cults already aimed if not at a fusion, then at least at a confrontation of the responsible and the orgiastic. The cave is a remnant of the subterranean gathering place of the mysteries; it is the womb of the Earth Mother. Plato's novel idea is the will to leave the womb of the Earth Mother and to follow the pure "path of light," that is, to *subordinate* (*podřídit*) the orgiastic entirely to responsibility. Hence the path of the Platonic soul leads directly to eternity and to the source of all eternity, the sun of "The Good." (104, my emphasis)

This subordination therefore takes the form of an "incorporation," whether that be understood in its psychoanalytic sense or in the wider sense of an integration that assimilates or retains within itself that which it exceeds, surpasses, or supersedes [*relève*]. The incorporation of one mystery by the other also amounts to an *incorporation* of one immortality within another, of one eternity within another. This enveloping of immortality would also correspond to a transaction between two negations or two disavowals of death. And in what amounts to a significant trait in the genealogy of responsibility, it will be marked by an internalization: by an individualization or subjectification, the soul's relation to itself as it falls back on itself in the very movement of incorporation:

> There is another aspect to this. The Platonic "conversion" makes a vision of the Good itself possible. This view is as unchanging and eternal as the Good itself. The journey after the Good, which is *the new* mystery *of the soul*, takes the form of *the soul's internal dialogue*. Immortality, inseparably linked with this dialogue, is thus different from the

immortality of the mysteries. *For the first time in history it is individual immortality, individual because inner,* inseparably bound up with its own achievement. Plato's doctrine of the immortality of the soul is the result of the confrontation of the orgiastic with responsibility. Responsibility triumphs over the orgiastic, *incorporates* it as a *subordinate* moment, as Eros which cannot understand itself until it understands that its origin is not in the corporeal world, in the cave, in the darkness, but rather that it is only a means for the ascent to the Good with its absolute claim and its hard *discipline.* (105, my emphasis)

Such a concept of *discipline* covers a number of senses. They all appear equally fundamental here: that of training first of all, or exercise, the idea of the work necessary to maintain control over orgiastic mystery, to have it work in its very subordination, like a slave or servant, in other words to set to work one secret by pressing it into service for another—but also to put the demonic secret of Eros to work within this new hierarchy. Secondly, this discipline is philosophy, or the dialectic, to the extent that it can be taught, precisely as a discipline, at the same time exoteric and esoteric; and thirdly, it is the exercise that consists in learning to die in order to attain the new immortality, that is, *meletē thanatou,* the care taken *with* death, the exercise *of* death, the "practicing (for) death" that Socrates speaks of in the *Phaedo.*

The *Phaedo* explicitly names philosophy: it is attentive anticipation of death, care brought to bear upon dying, meditation on the best way to receive, give, or give oneself death, experience of a *vigil* over the possibility of death, and over the possibility of death as impossibility. That very idea, namely this *meletē* or *epimeleia* that one can rightly translate by "care" or "solicitude," opens the vein—and begins the vigil—within which will be inscribed the sense that Heidegger confers on *Sorge* ("care") in *Being and Time.*[6] Let us think

6. Martin Heidegger, *Being and Time,* trans. John Macquarrie and Edward Robinson (New York: Harper and Row, 1962). Page references from this edition appear in brackets following paragraph and page numbers from the later German editions.

more precisely of the moment when Heidegger, however, following the tradition of the *cura* but without naming Plato, evokes only the *sollicitudo* of the Vulgate, Seneca and the *merimna* of the Stoics (§42, 199 [243]), which, nevertheless, *like* the Platonic *meletē*, also signifies care, concern, and solicitude.

The famous passage of the *Phaedo* (80e) that Patočka obliquely refers to but neither analyzes nor even cites, describes a sort of subjectivizing interiorization, the movement of the soul's gathering of itself, a fleeing of the body toward its interior where it withdraws into itself in order to recall itself to itself, in order to be next to itself, in order to keep itself in this gesture of re*member*ing. This conversion turns the soul around and amasses it upon itself. It is such a movement of gathering, as in the prefix *syn*, that announces the coming-to-conscience, as well as that representative conscience of the self by which the secret, but this time in the sense of the Latin *secretum* (from *secernere*)—separate, distinct, discerned—could be kept as an objective representation. For one of the threads we are following here is this history of secrecy and of its differentiated semantics, from the Greek mystical and cryptic to the Latin *secretum* and the German *Geheimnis*.

Socrates recalls a certain invisibility of the *psychē*, after having played again on *aïdēs-haidēs*, as he does in the *Cratylus*, on the fact that the invisible soul (*aidēs* also meaning "one who doesn't see," "blind") goes to its death *in the direction of* an invisible place that *is* also Hades (*Haidēs*), this invisibility of the *aïdēs* being in itself a figure of secrecy:

> If at its release the soul is pure and carries with it no contamination of the body [in other words Socrates describes this separation of the invisible soul, this secreting of the self by means of which the soul retreats from the visible body to assemble itself within itself, in order to be next to itself within its interior invisibility—separation and invisibility indeed being the criteria for secrecy], because it has never willingly associated with it in life (*ouden koinōnousa autō en tō biō hekousa einai*), but has shunned (*pheugousa*) it and kept itself separate (*synethroismenē hautēs eis heautēn*) as its

regular practice (*hate meletōsa aei touto*) [whenever Levinas refers to the *Phaedo*, as he often does in his different texts on death, he underlines this assembling of the soul upon itself as the moment when the self identifies with itself in its relation to death]—in other words, if it has pursued philosophy in the right way (*he orthōs philosophousa*) and really practiced how to face death easily (*kai tō onti tethnanai meletōsa rhadiōs*)—this is what "practicing death" means, isn't it (*ē ou tout' an eie meletē thanatou*)?[7]

This canonical passage is one of the most often cited, or at least evoked, in the history of philosophy. It is rarely subjected to a close reading. One might be surprised to learn that Heidegger doesn't quote it, in any case not once in *Being and Time*, not even in the passages devoted to care or to the being-toward-death. For it is indeed a matter of care,[8] a "keeping-vigil-for," a solicitude for death that constitutes the relation to self of that which, in existence, relates to oneself. For one never reinforces enough the fact that it is not the *psychē* that is there in the first place and that comes thereafter to care about its death, to keep watch over it, to be the very vigil of its death. No, the soul only distinguishes itself, separates itself, and assembles within itself in the experience of this *meletē tou thanatou*. It is nothing other than this care about dying as a relation to self and an assembling of self. It only returns to itself, in both senses of assembling itself and waking itself, becoming conscious [*s'éveiller*], in the sense of consciousness of self in general, through this care for death. And Patočka is quite right to speak here of mystery or secrecy in the constitution of a *psychē* or of an individual and responsible self. For it is thus that the soul separates itself in recalling itself to itself, and so it becomes individualized, interiorized,

---

7. Plato, *The Collected Dialogues*, ed. Edith Hamilton and Huntington Cairns (Princeton: Princeton University Press, 1999), 64. Greek added by Derrida following syntax of French translation.

8. In the discussion that follows I have translated Derrida's *souci* as "care/caring" in deference to the Heideggerian lexicon, even though "concern" might be a more usual equivalent and Derrida's first reference is generally to Plato's *meletē thanatou*.—Trans.

becomes its very invisibility. And hence it philosophizes from the beginning. Philosophy isn't something that comes to the soul by accident, for it is nothing other than this vigil over death that watches out for death and watches over death, as if over the very life of the soul. The *psychē* as life, as breath of life, as *pneuma*, only appears out of this caring anticipation of dying. The anticipation of this vigil already resembles a provisional mourning, a vigil [*veille*] as wake [*veillée*].

Whereas this vigil marks the event of a new secret, it incorporates within its discipline the orgiastic secret that it subordinates and renders dormant. Because of this *incorporation* or enveloping of demonic or orgiastic mystery, philosophy remains a sort of thaumaturgy even as it accedes to responsibility:

> In Neoplatonism the demonic—*Erōs* is a great *daimōn*—becomes a subservient realm in the eyes of the philosopher who has overcome all its temptations. Hence a somewhat unexpected outcome: the philosopher is at the same time a great *thaumaturge*. The Platonic philosopher is a magician [think of Socrates and his demon]—a Faustus. The Dutch historian of ideas, Gilles Quispel [Patočka refers here and elsewhere to the latter's book *Gnosis als Weltreligion*], derives from this one of the principal sources of the Faust legend and of Faustianism in general, that "endless striving" which makes Faust so dangerous but which can ultimately save him. (105)

Such a caring for death, an awakening that keeps vigil over death, a conscience that looks death in the face, is another name for freedom. There again, without wanting to neglect the essential differences, we can see in this link between the care of the being-toward-death, accepted in and of itself (*eigentlich*), and freedom, that is, responsibility, a structure analogous to that of the *Dasein* as described by Heidegger. Patočka is never far from Heidegger, in particular when he continues as follows:

> Another important moment is that the Platonic philosopher overcame death fundamentally by not fleeing from it

17

but by facing up to it. This philosophy was *meletē thanatou*, care for death; care for the soul is inseparable from care for death, which becomes the true (*pravá*) care for life; life (eternal) is born of this direct look at death, of an over-coming (*přemožení*) of death (*perhaps it is nothing but this "overcoming"*). That, however, together with the relation to the Good, identifying with the Good while breaking free of the demonic and the orgiastic, means *the rule of responsibility and so of freedom*. The soul is absolutely free, that is, it chooses its destiny. (105, my emphasis)

What is the significance of this allusion to the fact that "the rule of responsibility and so of freedom" consists perhaps of a triumph *over* death, in other words of a triumph of life (*The Triumph of Life*, Shelley would have called it, inverting the traditional figure of all the triumphs of death)?[9] Patočka even suggests in his parenthesis that all of that—so-called eternal life, responsibility, freedom—*is perhaps nothing other than* this triumph. Now a triumph retains traces of a struggle. It is as if a victory has been won in the course of a war between two fundamentally inseparable adversaries; the news rings out a day later at the time of the feast that commemo-rates (another wake) and preserves the memory of the war—this *polemos* that Patočka speaks of so often and grants so much im-portance in these *Heretical Essays*. The essay called "Wars of the Twentieth Century and the Twentieth Century as War" (119–37) is one of those that Ricoeur, in his preface to the French edition, judges "strange, frankly shocking" (viii). It involves a paradoxical phenomenology of darkness but also a secret covenant between night and day. Such a joining of opposites plays an essential role in Patočka's political thought, and although he cites only Ernst Jünger (*Der Arbeiter* [1932] and *Der Kampf als inneres Erlebnis* [1922]) and Teilhard de Chardin (*Writings in the Time of War* [1965]), his dis-course is at times close to Heidegger's very complicated and very equivocal discussion of the Heraclitean *polemos*, closer to it than

9. In the French translation of Patočka "overcoming" is *triomphe*. Cf. *Essais hérétiques sur la philosophie de l'histoire*, trans. Erika Abrams (Paris: Verdier, 1981).—Trans.

ever and, it seems to me, closer than Ricoeur avers in his preface, in spite of one essential difference that can't be elaborated upon here.[10]

War is a further experience of the gift of death [*la mort donnée*] (I put my enemy to death and I give my own life as a sacrifice by "dying for my country"). Patočka interprets the Heraclitean *polemos* in this way: rather than being an "expansion of 'life,'" it represents "the preponderance of the Night, of the will to the freedom of risk in the *aristeia*, holding one's own at the limit of human possibilities which the best choose when they opt for lasting fame in the memory of mortals in exchange for an ephemeral prolongation of a comfortable life" (136). This *polemos* unites adversaries; it brings together those who are opposed (Heidegger often insisted on the same thing). The *front*, as the site upon which the First World War was waged, provides a historic figure for this *polemos* that brings enemies together as though they were conjoined in the extreme proximity of the face-to-face. This exceptional and troubling glorification of the front perhaps presages another type of mourning, namely the loss of this front during and especially after the Second World War, the disappearance of this confrontation which allowed one to *identify* the enemy and even, and especially, to *identify with* the enemy. After the Second World War, as Patočka might say in the manner of Carl Schmitt, one loses the image or face of the enemy, one loses the war and perhaps, from then on, the very possibility of the political. Such an identification *of* the enemy, which, in the experience of the front, remains always very close to an identification *with* the enemy, is what troubles and fascinates Patočka more than anything else.

> That is the same sentiment, the same vision which Teilhard sees before him when he experiences the superhuman divine at the front line. And Jünger writes at one place that the combatants in an attack become two parts of a single force, fusing into a single body, and adds: "Into a single body—an odd comparison. Whoever understands it

10. I deal with that question in "Heidegger's Ear: Philopolemology (*Geschlecht* IV)," in *Reading Heidegger: Commemorations*, ed. John Sallis (Bloomington: Indiana University Press, 1993).

affirms both self and the enemy, lives at once in the whole and in the part. That person then can think the gods who let these colored threads slip between their fingers—with a smiling face" [*Der Kampf als inneres Erlebnis*].—Is it an accident that two of the most profound thinkers of the front-line experience, so different in other respects, arrive independently at comparisons which revive Heraclitus' vision of being as *polemos*? Or does something open up to us therein of the meaning of the history of western humanity which will not be denied and which today is becoming the meaning of history as such? (136–37)

But if it commemorates death and victory over death, such a triumph also marks the moment of jubilation of the grieving survivor who enjoys their survival or surfeit of life [*sur-vie*] in an almost maniacal way, as Freud pointed out. In this genealogy of responsibility and of freedom, of their "reign" as Patočka calls it, the triumphant affirmation of the free and responsible self on the part of a mortal or finite being can indeed be expressed maniacally. Thus, in the same disavowal, it would hide, from others or from itself, more than one secret: that of the orgiastic mystery that it has enslaved, subordinated, and incorporated, and that of its own mortality that it refuses or denies in the very experience of its triumph.

Such a genealogy thus seems indeed ambiguous. The interpretation of this philosophical or philosophico-political emergence of absolute freedom ("the soul is absolutely free, that is, it chooses its destiny" [105]) seems nothing less than straightforward and self-sufficient; but it betrays a disquieting assessment of things. For in spite of the implicit praise for the responsible freedom that awakes from its orgiastic or demonic sleep, Patočka recognizes in this vigilance a "new mythology." Although it is incorporated, disciplined, subjugated, and enslaved, the orgiastic is not annihilated. It continues to motivate subterraneously a mythology of responsible freedom that is at the same time a politics, indeed the still partly intact foundation of politics in the West; it continues to motivate such a freedom after the second reversal or conversion that is Christianity:

So a new, light mythology of the soul grows on the basis of the duality of the *authentic* (*pravé*)/responsible and the exceptional/orgiastic: the orgiastic *is not removed but is disciplined and made subservient* (*není odstraněno, ale zkázněno a učiněno služebným*). (106, my emphasis)

One can recognize the proximity to Heidegger throughout Patočka's discourse, both here and elsewhere, but the differences between them, whether explicit or potential, are nonetheless significant. The theme of authenticity, the links among care, being-toward-death, freedom and responsibility, the very idea of a genesis or a history of egological subjectivity, all such ideas certainly have a Heideggerian flavor to them. But this genealogy is hardly Heideggerian in style when it takes into account an incorporation of an earlier mystery that blurs the limits of every epoch. Without wanting at all costs to assign Patočka a particular heritage, one might say that certain of his genealogist tendencies at times seem more Nietzschean than Husserlian or Heideggerian. Moreover, Patočka cites Nietzsche's reference to Christianity as the Platonism of the people. Such an idea has "truth in it" (107), he notes, up to a certain point. The difference, which is not negligible or rather which is *nothing* itself, resides in that idea's horrifying abyssality.

If the orgiastic remains enveloped, if the demonic persists, incorporated and dominated, in a new experience of responsible freedom, then the latter never becomes what it is. It will never become pure and authentic, or absolutely new. The Platonic philosopher is in no better a position than the animal when it comes to "looking" death in the face and, as a result, to having access to that authenticity of existence linked to the *epimeleia tēs psykhēs* as *meletē thanatou*, the caring concern for the soul that cares by watching for/over death. By virtue of its very possibility, this doubling of secrecy or mystery now blurs all the limits that form the major outlines of Heidegger's existential analytic. There is first of all demonic mystery in itself, one might say. Then there is the structure of secrecy that keeps that mystery hidden, incorporated, concealed but alive, in the structure of free responsibility that claims to go beyond it and that in fact only succeeds by subordinating mystery and keeping it subjugated. The secret of responsibility would consist in keeping secret, or "incorporated," the secret of the demonic, thus protecting within itself a nucleus of irresponsibility or of absolute unconsciousness, something Patočka will later call "orgiastic irresponsibility" (112).

In hypothesizing the moment that Patočka identifies as that of the Platonic philosopher, we could perhaps recover the semantic difference between mystery and what should more strictly be called secrecy, the *secretum* whose sense points toward a separation (*se-cernere*) and more generally toward the objective representation that the conscious subject keeps within itself: what it knows, what it knows how to represent to itself, even though it cannot or will not declare or avow that representation. The *secretum* supposes the constitution of this liberty of the soul as the conscience of a responsible subject. In short, waking from demonic *mystery*, surpassing the demonic, means acceding to the possibility of the *secretum*, of the keeping of a secret. For it also involves gaining access to the individualization of the relation to oneself, to the ego that separates itself from the community of fusion. But this simply means exchanging one secret for another. A particular economy happily sacrifices a mystery for a secret within a history of truth as history of dissimulation, within a genealogy that is a cryptology or general *mystology*.

All that derives therefore from a mythomorphic or mythopoetic *incorporation*. In formalizing and in rigidifying a little the lines of Patočka's argument, without, for all that, I hope, betraying it, I would hold that, in the first place, he simply describes the Platonic incorporation of demonic mystery and orgiastic irresponsibility. But can one not go further and say that this incorporation is in turn *repressed* by a certain Christianity, in the precise moment that Patočka calls the Christian *reversal?* One would thus be tempted to distinguish two economies, or one economy with two systems: *incorporation* and *repression*.

The essentially political dimension of this crypto- or mystogenealogy becomes clearer. It seems to be what is at stake in this passage from Platonic secrecy (containing its incorporated demonic mystery) to the Christian secret as *mysterium tremendum*. In order to examine this it will be necessary to distinguish three important motifs in this genealogy that combines secrecy with responsibility.

1. One must never forget, and precisely for political reasons, that the mystery that is incorporated then repressed is never destroyed. This genealogy has an axiom, namely that history never effaces what it buries; it always keeps within itself the secret of whatever it encrypts, the secret of its secret. This is a secret history of kept secrets. For that reason the genealogy is also an economy. Orgiastic mystery recurs indefinitely; it is always at work: not only in Platonism, as we have seen, but also in Christianity and even in the space of the *Aufklärung* and of secularization. Patočka encourages us to learn a political lesson from this, one for today and tomorrow, by reminding us that every revolution, whether atheistic or religious, bears witness to a return of the sacred in the form of enthusiasm or fervor, otherwise known as the presence of the gods within us. Speaking of this "new flood of the orgiastic" (113), something that remains forever imminent and that corresponds to an abdication of responsibility, Patočka gives the example of the religious fervor that took hold during the French Revolution. Given the affinity between the sacred and secrecy, and between ceremonies of sacrifice and initiation, it might be said that all revolutionary fervor produces its slogans as though they were sacrificial rites or effects of secrecy. Patočka doesn't say that expressly, but his quotation from Durkheim seems to point in that direction:

> The aptitude of society for setting itself up as a god or for creating gods was never more apparent than during the first years of the French Revolution. At that time, in fact, under the influence of the general enthusiasm, things purely laical by nature were transformed by public opinion into sacred things: these were the Fatherland, Liberty, Reason.

And after that quote from *The Elementary Forms of the Religious Life*,[11] Patočka continues:

11. Emile Durkheim, *The Elementary Forms of the Religious Life*, trans. Joseph Ward Swain (New York: The Free Press, 1965), 244–45.

That, to be sure, is an enthusiasm which, for all the cult of reason, has an orgiastic cast, either undisciplined or insufficiently disciplined by a link to personal responsibility. Here a danger of a new decline into the orgiastic is acutely evident. (113)

Such a warning can, of course, only oppose one form of mourning to another (such are the paradoxes or aporias of every economy), melancholy to triumph or triumph to melancholy, one form of depression to another form of depression, or, and this amounts to the same thing, one form of depression to a form of resistance to depression. We escape the demonic orgiastic by means of the Platonic triumph, and we escape the latter by means of the sacrifice or repentance of the Christian "reversal," that is, by means of the Christian "repression."

2. If it is not exaggerating to incline this interpretation of the *epimeleia tēs psykhēs* toward a psychoanalytic economy of secrecy as mourning or of mourning as secrecy, I would say that what separates that economy from Heidegger's influence is its essential Christianity. Heideggerian thought was not simply a constant attempt, conducted with some difficulty, to separate itself from Christianity (a gesture that always needs to be related—however complex this relation—to the incredible unleashing of anti-Christian violence represented by Nazism's most official and explicit ideology, something one tends to forget these days). The same Heideggerian thinking often consists, notably in certain determining motifs of *Sein und Zeit*, in repeating on an ontological level Christian themes and texts that have been "de-Christianized." Such themes and texts are then presented as ontic, anthropological, or contrived attempts that come to a sudden halt on the way to an ontological recovery of their own originary possibility (whether that be, for example, the *status corruptionis*, the difference between authentic and inauthentic or the fall [*Verfallen*] into the *They*, whether it be *sollicitudo* and care, the pleasure of seeing and of curiosity, of the authentic or vulgar concept of time, of the texts of the Vulgate, of Saint Augustine or of Kierkegaard). It is as if Patočka makes an inverse yet symmetrical gesture, which perhaps therefore amounts to the same thing,

reontologizing the historic themes of Christianity and attributing to revelation or to the *mysterium tremendum* the ontological content that Heidegger attempts to remove from it.

3. But it is not as if Patočka does this in order to redirect things along the path of an orthodox Christianity. His own heresy perhaps intersects with what one might call, a little provocatively, that other heresy, namely the twisting or diverting by which, in its own way, the Heideggerian repetition affects Christianity.

On two or three occasions Patočka denounces the persistence of a type of Platonism—and of a type of Platonic politics—at the heart of European Christianity. For, in short, the latter has not sufficiently repressed Platonism in the course of its reversal, and still mouths its words. In this sense, and from the political point of view, Nietzsche's idea of Christianity as the Platonism of the people would once more be reinforced (found, up to a certain point, to have "truth in it," as we were saying just now).

A. *On the one hand*, for Patočka responsible decision-making is subjected to knowledge:

> Christian theology rejected the Platonic solution [it condemns the orgiastic, certainly, but on the basis of a metaphysics of knowledge as *sophia tou kosmou*: knowledge of the order of the world and subordination of ethics and politics to objective knowledge], though this theology did accept extensive elements of a solution launched along Platonic lines.
>
> Platonic rationalism, the Platonic effort to subject even responsibility itself to the objectivity of knowledge, continues to affect the nether layers (*v podzemí*) of the Christian conception. Theology itself rests on a "natural" foundation, understanding "the supernatural" as a fulfillment of "the natural." (110)

To "subject even responsibility itself to the objectivity of knowledge" is obviously, in Patočka's view, to discount responsibility. And how can we not subscribe to what he is implying here? Saying that a responsible decision must be made on the basis of knowledge seems to define the condition of possibility of responsibility (one cannot make a responsible decision without science or conscience, without knowing what one is doing, for what reasons, in view of what, and under what conditions), at the same time as it defines the condition of impossibility of this same responsibility (if decision-making is relegated to a knowledge that it is content to follow or to develop, then it is no more a responsible decision; it is the technical deployment of a cognitive apparatus, the simple mechanistic deployment of a theorem). This *aporia of responsibility* would thus define the relation between Platonic and Christian paradigms throughout the history of morality and politics.

B. That is why, *on the other hand*, although Patočka inscribes his ethical or legal, and in particular his political, discourse within the perspective of a Christian eschatology, he manages to outline some of what remains "unthought" in Christianity. Whether ethical or political, the Christian consciousness of responsibility is incapable of reflecting on the Platonic thinking that it represses, and at the same time it is incapable of reflecting on the orgiastic mystery that Platonic thinking incorporates. That appears in the definition of that which is precisely the place and subject of every responsibility, namely the *person*. Immediately after describing the Christian "reversal" or "repression" in the *mysterium tremendum*, Patočka writes,

> In the final analysis [of Christian mystery], the soul is not a relation to an object, however noble (like the Platonic Good) [which implies, therefore, "such as in Platonism where it is the relation to a transcendent Good that also governs the ideal order of the Greek *polis* or the Roman *civitas*"], but rather to a Person who sees into the soul without being accessible to view. What a Person is, that really is not adequately thematized in the Christian perspective. (107)

The inadequacy of this thematization comes to rest on the threshold of responsibility. It doesn't thematize what a responsible person *is*, that is, what it *must be*, namely this exposing of the soul to the gaze of another person, of a person as transcendent other, as an other who looks at me, but who looks without the-subject-who-says-I being able to reach that other, see her, hold her within the reach of my gaze. And let us not forget that an inadequate thematization of what responsibility is or *must be* is also an *irresponsible* thematization: not knowing, having neither sufficient knowledge nor consciousness of what being *responsible* means, is of itself a lack of responsibility. In order to be responsible it is necessary to respond to or answer to what being responsible means. For if it is true that the concept of responsibility has, throughout a history that is as consistent as it is continuous, always implied involvement in action, doing, a *praxis*, a *decision* that exceeds simple conscience or simple theoretical understanding, it is also true that the same concept requires a decision or responsible action to answer for itself *consciously*, that is, with knowledge of a thematics of what is done, of what action signifies, its causes, ends, etc. In debates concerning responsibility one must always take into account this original and irreducible complexity that links theoretical consciousness (which must also be a thetic or thematic consciousness) to "practical" conscience (ethical, legal, political), if only to avoid the arrogance of so many "clean consciences." We must continually remind ourselves that some part of irresponsibility insinuates itself wherever one demands responsibility without sufficiently conceptualizing and thematically thinking what "responsibility" means; *that is to say everywhere*. One can say *everywhere* a priori and nonempirically, for if the complex linkage between the theoretical and practical that we just referred to is, quite clearly, irreducible, then the heterogeneity between the two linked orders is just as irreducible. As a result, the activating of responsibility (decision, act, *praxis*) will always have to extend behind and beyond any theoretical or thematic determination. It will have to decide without it, independently from knowledge; that will be the condition of a practical idea of freedom. We should therefore conclude that not only is the thematization of the concept of responsibility always inadequate, but that it will always be so because it must be so. And what goes here for responsibility also goes, for the same reasons, for freedom and for decision.

The heterogeneity whose outline we see here between the exercise of responsibility and its theoretical, or even doctrinal, thematization, is also, surely, what ties responsibility to *heresy*, to *hairesis* as choice, election, preference, inclination, bias, that is, decision; but also as a school (philosophical, religious, literary) that corresponds to that bias; and finally heresy in the sense fixed in the vocabulary of the Catholic Church and made more general since, namely, divergence within a doctrine, divergence within and with respect to it, with reference to an officially and publicly stated doctrine and the institutional community that is governed by it. Now, to the extent that this heresy always marks a divergence or departure [*écart*], keeping itself *apart from* what is publicly or commonly declared, it isn't only, in its very possibility, the essential condition of responsibility; paradoxically, it also destines responsibility to the resistance or dissidence of a type of secrecy. It keeps responsibility apart [*tient la responsabilité à l'écart*] and in secret. And responsibility *insists on* what is apart [*tient à l'écart*] and kept secret.

Dissidence, divergence, heresy, resistance, secrecy—so many experiences that are paradoxical in the strong sense that Kierkegaard gives to the word. In fact it comes down to linking secrecy to a responsibility that consists, according to the most convinced and convincing *doxa*, in *responding*, hence in answering to the other, before the other and before the law, and if possible publicly, answering for itself, its intentions, its aims, and for the name of the agent deemed responsible. This relation between responsibility and responding is not common to all languages, but it does exist in Czech (*odpovědnost*).

What I have said might seem faithful to the spirit of Patočka's heresy at the same time as it is heretical with respect to that very heresy. The paradox can in fact be interpreted directly from what Patočka maintains concerning the person and concerning the Christian *mysterium tremendum*, but also against it, in that when he speaks of an inadequate thematization he seems to appeal to some ultimate adequacy of thematization that could be accomplished. On the other hand, the theme of thematization, the sometimes phenomenological motif of thematic conscience, is the thing that is, if not denied, at least strictly limited in its pertinence by that other more radical form of responsibility that exposes me dissymmetrically to the gaze of the other; where my gaze, precisely as regards me [*ce qui me regarde*], is no longer the measure of all things. The concept of responsibility is one of those strange concepts that give food for thought without giving themselves over to thematization. It presents itself neither as a theme nor as a thesis, it gives without allowing itself to be seen [*sans se donner à voir*], without presenting itself in person by means of a "fact of being seen" that can be phenomenologically intuited. This paradoxical concept also has the structure of a type of secret—what is called, in the code of certain religious practices, mystery. The exercise of responsibility seems to leave no choice but this one, however uncomfortable it be, of paradox, heresy, and secrecy. More serious still, it must always run the risk of conversion and apostasy: there is no responsibility without a dissident and inventive rupture with respect to tradition, authority, orthodoxy, rule, or doctrine.

The dissymmetry of the gaze, this disproportion that relates me, in whatever concerns me, to a gaze that I don't see and that remains secret from me although it commands me, is the terrifying, dreadful, *tremendous* mystery that, according to Patočka, is manifested in Christian mystery. Such dread has no place in the transcendent experience that relates Platonic responsibility to the *agathon*; nor in the politics that is so instituted. But the terror of this secret spreads, exceeding and preceding the complacent relation of a subject to an object.

Is the reference to this abyssal dissymmetry in the exposure to the gaze of the other a motif that derives firstly and uniquely from Christianity, even if it be from an inadequately thematized Christianity? Let us leave aside the question of whether one finds at least its equivalent "before" or "after" the Gospels, in Judaism or in Islam. If we restrict ourselves to reading what Patočka writes, we can in any case have no doubt that in his view Christianity—and the Christian Europe that he never dissociates from it—provides the most powerful momentum for plumbing the depths of this abyss of responsibility, even if it is limited by the weight of what remains unthought, in particular its incorrigible Platonism:

> By virtue of this foundation (*základ*) in the abyssal deepening of the soul, Christianity remains thus far the greatest,

unsurpassed but also un-thought-through human outreach
that enabled humans to struggle against decadence. (108)

One should understand that in saying that this "outreach" has not
been thought through, Patočka intends that such a task be taken to
its conclusion; not only by means of a more thorough thematization but also by means of a political and historical implementation
or action; and he advocates that along the lines of a messianic eschatology that is nevertheless indissociable from phenomenology.
Something has not yet arrived, neither at Christianity nor by means
of Christianity. What has not yet arrived at, or happened to, Christianity is Christianity. Christianity has not yet come to Christianity. What has not yet come about is the fulfillment, within history
and in political history, and first and foremost in European politics,
of the new responsibility announced by the *mysterium tremendum*.
There has not yet been an authentically Christian politics because
there remains this residue of the Platonic polis. Christian politics
must break more radically with Greco-Roman Platonic politics in
order to finally fulfill the *mysterium tremendum*. Only on this condition will Europe have a future, and will there be a future in general,
for Patočka speaks less of a past event or fact than he does of a
promise. The promise has already been made. The time of such a
promise defines both the experience of the *mysterium tremendum*
and the double repression that institutes it, the *double repression* by
means of which it represses but retains within itself *both* the orgiastic incorporated by Platonism *and* Platonism itself.

What is implicit yet explosive in Patočka's text can be extended *in
a radical way*, for it is heretical with respect to a certain Christianity
and a certain Heideggerianism but also with respect to all the important European discourses. Taken to its extreme, the text seems
to suggest on the one hand that Europe will not be what it must be
until it becomes fully Christian, until the *mysterium tremendum* is
adequately thematized. On the other hand, it also suggests that the
Europe to come must no longer be Greek, Greco-Platonic, or even
Roman. The most radical insistence promised by the *mysterium tremendum* would be upon a Europe so new (or so old) that it would
be freed from the Greek or Roman memory that is so commonly

invoked in speaking of it; freed to the extent of breaking all ties with this memory, becoming heterogeneous to it. What would be the secret of a Europe emancipated from both Athens and Rome?

In the first place there is the enigma of an impossible and inevitable transition, that from Platonism to Christianity. We should not be surprised to notice that in the moment of reversal or repression a privileged status is accorded the unstable, multiple, and somewhat spectral historic figure (one that becomes all the more fascinating and exciting) that is called Neoplatonism, and notably whatever relates this Neoplatonism to the political power of Rome. But Patočka not only refers to the political profile of Neoplatonism; he also makes oblique reference to something that is not a thing but that is probably the very site of the most decisive paradox, namely the *gift that is not a present*, the gift of something that remains inaccessible, unpresentable, and as a consequence secret. The event of this gift would link the essence without essence of the gift to secrecy. For one might say that a gift that could be recognized as such in the light of day, a gift destined for recognition, would immediately annul itself. The gift is the secret itself, if the secret *itself* can be told. Secrecy is the last word of the gift which is the last word of the secret.

Discussion concerning the passage from Plato to Christianity immediately follows the allusion to the "new, light mythology of the soul [that] grows on the basis of the duality of the authentic/responsible and the exceptional/orgiastic." Patočka then states that "the orgiastic is not removed but is disciplined and made subservient," and continues,

> It is understandable that this entire complex of motifs could not but acquire a global significance in the moment when the end of the *polis/civitas* in the form of the Roman principality posed the problem of a new responsibility founded on the transcendent even within the framework of the social, in relation to a state which could no longer be a community of equals in freedom. Freedom is no longer defined in terms of a relationship to equals (other citizens) but to a transcendent Good. That also poses new questions

and makes new solutions possible. The social problem of the Roman Empire is ultimately acted out on a foundation made possible by the Platonic conception of the soul.

The Neoplatonic philosopher Julian the Apostate on the imperial throne represents—as Quispel saw, probably rightly—an important turn in the relation between the orgiastic and the discipline of responsibility. Christianity could overcome this Platonic solution only *by an about-face*. Responsible life was itself presented as a *gift* from something which ultimately, though it has the character of the Good, has also the traits of the *inaccessible* (*nepřístupného*) and forever superior to humans—the traits of the *mysterium* that always has the final word. Christianity, after all, understands the good differently than Plato—as a self-forgetting goodness and a *self-denying* (not orgiastic) love. (106, my emphasis)

Let us hold on to the word "gift." Between on the one hand this denial that involves renouncing the self, this abnegation of the gift, of goodness, or of the generosity of the gift that must withdraw, hide, and also in effect sacrifice itself in order to give, and on the other hand the repression that would transform the gift into an economy of sacrifice, is there not a secret affinity, an unavoidable risk of contamination of two possibilities as close one to the other as they are heterogeneous? For what is given in this trembling, in the actual trembling of dread, is nothing other than death itself, a new significance for death, a new apprehension of death, a new way in which to give oneself death or to put oneself to death [*se donner la mort*]. The difference between Platonism and Christianity would be above all "the turn in the face of death and death eternal; [a soul] which lives in anxiety and hope inextricably intertwined, which trembles in the knowledge of its sin and with its whole being offers itself in the sacrifice of penance" (108). Such is the rupture that functions in the mode of, and within the limits of, a repression: between the metaphysics, ethics, and politics of the Platonic Good (that is, the "incorporated" orgiastic mystery) and the *mysterium tremendum* of Christian responsibility:

It is not the orgiastic—that remains not only subordinated but, in certain respects, suppressed to the limit—yet it is still a *mysterium tremendum*. *Tremendum*, for responsibility is now vested not in a humanly comprehensible essence of goodness and unity but, rather, in an inscrutable relation to the absolute highest being in whose hands we are not externally, but internally. (106)

Since he knows Heidegger's thought and language so well, Patočka's allusion is made with quite conscious intent. He speaks of a supreme being, of God as one who, holding me from within, in his hands and within his gaze, defines everything regarding me, and so rouses me to responsibility. The definition of God as supreme being is the ontotheological proposition that Heidegger rejects when he speaks of the originary and essential responsibility of the *Dasein*. Within the hearing of this call (*Ruf*), on the basis of which it is experienced as originally responsible, guilty (*schuldig*), or indebted before any fault in particular and before any determined debt, the *Dasein* is in the first place not responsible to any determined being who looks at it or speaks to it. When Heidegger describes what he names the call or the sense of calling (*Rufsinn*) as experience of care and original phenomenon of the *Dasein* in its originary being-responsible or being-guilty (*Schuldigsein*), the existential analysis that he is proposing claims to go beyond any theological perspective (§54, 269 [313]). This originarity does not imply any relation of the *Dasein* to a supreme being as origin of the voice that speaks to the *Gewissen*, or conscience, or as origin of the gaze before which moral conscience must stand; in fact it excludes such a relation. On several occasions Heidegger describes the Kantian representation of the tribunal, *before* which or *in whose sight* conscience is summoned to appear, as an image (*Bild*), thereby disqualifying it at least from an ontological point of view (§55, 271 [316]; §59, 293 [339]). On the other hand, the silent voice that calls the *Dasein* guards itself against any possible identification. It is absolutely indeterminate, even if "the peculiar indefiniteness of the caller and the impossibility of making more definite what this caller is, are not just nothing" (*Die eigentümliche Unbestimmtheit und Unbestimmbarkeit*

33

des Rufers ist nicht nichts) (§57, 275 [319]). The origin of responsibility does not in any way reduce, originarily, to a supreme being. But there is no mystery in that. Nor any secret. There is no mystery to this indetermination and indeterminacy. The fact that the voice remains silent and is not the voice of anyone in particular, of any determinable identity, is the condition of the *Gewissen* (that which is translated loosely as moral conscience—let us call it the responsible conscience), but that in no way implies that this voice is a secret or "mysterious voice" (*geheimnisvolle Stimme*) (§56, 274 [318]).

Thus Patočka deliberately takes an opposite tack to Heidegger. He is no doubt convinced that there is no true binding responsibility or obligation that doesn't come from someone, from a person such as an absolute being who transfixes me, takes possession of me, holds me in its hands and in its gaze (even though through this dissymmetry I don't see it; it is essential that I don't see it). This supreme being, this infinite other first comes across me, it falls upon me (it is true that Heidegger also says that the call whose source remains indeterminable comes from me while falling upon me, it comes out of me as it comes across me—"Der Ruf kommt aus mir und doch über mich" [§57, 275 (320)]). While seeming to contradict Heidegger by assigning the origin of my responsibility to a supreme being, Patočka also seems to contradict himself, for he says elsewhere that Nietzsche was quite correct in describing Christianity as the Platonism of the people because "the Christian God took over the transcendence of the onto-theological conception as a matter of course," whereas on the other hand there is "a fundamental, profound difference" (107) between Christianity and ontotheology. In order to escape this contradiction he will need— and this is probably an implicit project of Patočka's discourse—to keep his thinking of a supreme being distinct from all ontotheology in the sense that Heidegger, and Heidegger alone, gave to the term and whose concept he sought to legitimize.

The crypto- or mystogenealogy of responsibility is woven with the double and inextricably intertwined thread of the gift and of death: in short of the *gift of death*. The gift made to me by God to the extent that he holds me in his gaze and in his hands while at the same time remaining inaccessible to me, the terribly dissymmetrical gift of the *mysterium tremendum*, only allows me to respond and only rouses me to the responsibility it gives me by making a gift of death [*en me donnant la mort*], giving the secret of death, a new experience of death.

The question of whether this discourse on the gift and on the gift of death is or is not a discourse on sacrifice and on *dying for the other* is something that we must now analyze. Especially since this investigation into the secret of responsibility, into the paradoxical covenant between secrecy and responsibility, is eminently historical and political. It concerns the very essence or future of European politics.

Like the polis and the Grecian politics that corresponds to it, the Platonic moment incorporates demonic mystery in vain; it introduces or *presents* itself as a moment without mystery. What distinguishes the moment of the Platonic polis both from the orgiastic mystery that it incorporates *and* from the Christian *mysterium tremendum* that represses it, is the fact that in the first case one openly declares that secrecy will not be allowed. There is a place for secrecy, for the *mysterium*, or for the mystical in what *precedes* or what *follows* Platonism (demonic orgiastic mystery or *mysterium tremendum*); but according to Patočka there is none such in the philosophy and politics of the Platonic tradition. That sense of the political excludes the mystical. Thenceforth, for Europe, and even in modern Europe, to inherit this politics of Greco-Platonic provenance is to neglect, repress, or exclude from itself every essential possibility of secrecy and every link between responsibility and the keeping of a secret; everything that allows responsibility to be dedicated to secrecy. From there it takes very little, a single step, to envisage an inevitable passage from the *democratic* (in the Greek sense) to the *totalitarian*; it is the simple process that takes place once such a passage is opened. The consequences will be most serious; they deserve a second look.

TWO

Beyond: Giving for the Taking, Teaching and
Learning to Give, Death *[Au-delà: Donner à prendre,
apprendre à donner—la mort]*

This narrative is genealogical but it does not simply amount to an
act of memory. It *witnesses*, in the manner of an ethical or political
act, for today and for tomorrow. It means first of all thinking about
what takes place today. The orientation of the narrative follows a
genealogical detour in order to describe the current European return of mystery and orgiastic mystification; in order to describe it
but more particularly to denounce, deplore, and combat it.

As the title of his essay indicates, Patočka asks why technological civilization is in decline (*úpadková*). The answer seems clear:
this fall into inauthenticity indicates a return of the orgiastic or
demonic. Contrary to what is normally thought, technological mo-
dernity doesn't neutralize anything; it causes a certain form of the
demonic to re-emerge. Of course, it does neutralize also, through
indifference and boredom, but because of that, and precisely to the
same extent, it allows the return of the demonic. There is an affinity, or at least a synchrony, between a culture of boredom and an
orgiastic one. The domination of technology encourages demonic
irresponsibility, and the sexual force of the latter does not need
to be emphasized. All that occurs against the background of this
boredom that acts in concert with a technological leveling effect.
Technological civilization produces a heightening or mobilization

of the orgiastic, with the familiar accompanying effects of aestheticism and individualism, but only to the extent that it also produces
boredom, for it "levels" or neutralizes the mysterious or irreplaceable uniqueness of the responsible self. The individualism of technological civilization relies precisely on a misunderstanding of the
unique self. It is the individualism of a *role* and not of a *person*. In
other words it might be called the individualism of a masque or
persona, a character [*personnage*] and not a person. Patočka reminds
us of interpretations—especially that of Burckhardt—according to
which modern individualism, as it has developed since the Renais-
sance, concerns itself with the *role that is played* rather than with
this unique person whose secret remains hidden behind the social
mask.

The alternatives are confused: individualism becomes socialism
or collectivism, it simulates an ethics or politics of singularity; liber-
alism joins socialism, democracy joins totalitarianism, and all these
figures share the same indifference concerning anything but the objectivity of the role. Equality for all, the slogan of bourgeois revolution, becomes the objective or quantifiable equality of roles, not of
persons.

This critique of the mask clearly harks back to a tradition, especially when it is part of a denunciation of technology in the name of
an originary authenticity. Patočka is doubtless somewhat insensitive to how consistent a tradition it is, its logic seeming to continue
unperturbed from Plato to Heidegger. And just as the role played
hides the authenticity of the irreplaceable self behind a social mask,
so the civilization of boredom produced by techno-scientific objectivity hides mystery: "The most sophisticated inventions are boring
if they do not lead to an exacerbation of the Mystery (*Tajemství*)
concealed by what we discover, what is revealed to us" (114).

Let us outline the logic of this discourse. It criticizes an inauthentic dissimulation (that is the sense common to technology,
role-playing, individualism, and boredom) not in the name of a
revelation or truth as unveiling, but in the name of another dissimulation that, in what it holds back [*dans sa réserve même*], keeps
the mystery veiled. Inauthentic dissimulation, that of the masked
role, bores to the extent that it claims to unveil, show, expose,

exhibit, and excite curiosity. By unveiling everything, it hides that whose essence resides in its remaining hidden, namely the authentic mystery of the person. Authentic mystery must *remain* mysterious, and we should approach it only by letting it be what it is in truth, namely veiled, withdrawn, dissimulated. Authentic dissimulation is inauthentically dissimulated by the violence of unveiling. The words "mystery" or "fundamental mystery" appear a number of times in the final pages of the article, and their logic and intonation, at least, seem more and more Heideggerian.

Yet another concept could well represent the most decisive recourse here, that of force (*síla*). Everything Patočka tends to discredit—inauthenticity, technology, boredom, individualism, masks, roles—derives from a "metaphysics of force" (*Metafyzika síly*, 116). Force has become the modern figure of being. Being has allowed itself to be determined as a calculable force; and man, instead of relating to the being that is *hidden under* this figure of force, represents himself as quantifiable power. Patočka describes this definition of being as force by means of a schema that is analogous to that employed by Heidegger in his texts on technology:

> Humans have ceased to be a relation to Being (*Bytí*) and have become a force, a mighty one, one of the mightiest. [This superlative (*jednou z nejmocnějších*) indeed signifies that man has placed himself in a homogeneous relation with the forces of the world, but simply as the strongest among those forces.] Especially in their social being, they became a gigantic transformer, releasing cosmic forces accumulated and bound over the eons. It seems as if humans have become a grand energy accumulator in a world of sheer forces, on the one hand making use of those forces to exist and multiply, yet on the other hand themselves integrated into the same process, accumulated, calculated, utilized, and manipulated like any other state of energy. (116)

This description might at first seem Heideggerian, as do a number of other formulations such as "Hidden within force there is Being" (ibid.) or "Thus force manifests itself as the highest concealment of Being" (117). The same can be said for the interpretation of the dissimulation of being as force, and the dissimulation of being in the entity. One might say that Patočka doesn't shy away from such a reading even if the only explicit reference to Heidegger takes a strangely encrypted form. Heidegger is merely *alluded to* as though, for one reason or another, he is not to be named (whereas others like Hannah Arendt are named, in the same context and to make a similar point). For example: "A great contemporary thinker presented this vision of being absorbed in what is in his work without being trusted or noted" (ibid.). Heidegger is there, but he is not paid any attention. He is visible but not seen. Heidegger is there like a purloined letter, he seems to say, although not in so many words. We shall shortly witness the return of this purloined letter.

There are, however, formulations that Heidegger would never have subscribed to, for example, that which presents this metaphysics of force as "mythological," or again as an inauthentic fiction: "Thus a metaphysics of force is fictitious and inauthentic [*fiktivní a nepravá*—untrue]" (116). Heidegger would never have said that metaphysical determinations of being or the history of the dissimulation of being in the figures or modes of the entity developed as *myths* or *fictions*. Such terms would be more Nietzschean than Heideggerian. And Heidegger would never have said that metaphysics as such was of itself "untrue" or "inauthentic."

However, if one holds to the logic of (inauthentic) dissimulation that dissimulates (authentic) dissimulation by means of the simple gesture of exposing or exhibiting it, of seeing in order to see or having it seen in order to see (which is Heidegger's definition of "curiosity"), then one has here an example of a logic of secrecy. It is never better kept than in being exposed. Dissimulation is never better dissimulated than by means of this particular kind of dissimulation that consists in making a show of exposing it, unveiling it, laying it bare. The mystery of being is dissimulated by this inauthentic dissimulation that consists in exposing being as a force, showing it behind its mask, behind its fiction or its simulacrum. Is it therefore surprising to see Patočka evoke Poe's "Purloined Letter"?

Thus force manifests itself as the highest concealment of Being which, like the purloined letter in E. A. Poe's familiar story, is safest where it is exposed to view in the form of the totality of what-is; that is, of forces that organize and release one another, not excluding humans who, like all else, are stripped of all mystery.

A great contemporary thinker presented this vision of being absorbed in what is in his work without being trusted or noted. (117)

Heidegger *himself*, and his work, come to resemble a purloined letter: not only interpreting the play of dissimulation as the practice of exposing letters, but appearing in the place of what is called here being or the letter [*l'être ou lettre*]. This is not the first time that Heidegger and Poe have been found under the same cover, folded together, for better or for worse, indeed quite posthumously, in the same (hi)story of letters. Patočka takes it further, warning us of this sleight of hand while also keeping Heidegger's name under wraps, performing one trick to hide another.

Since the fact of death is essential to the play of "The Purloined Letter," we are brought back to the *apprehension of death*, namely this way of *giving oneself death* that seems to imprint upon this heretical essay its dominant impulse.

What we are here calling the apprehension of death refers as much to the concern, anxious solicitude, care taken for the soul (*epimeleia tēs psykhēs*) in the *meletē thanatou*, as it does to the meaning given to death by the interpretative attitude that, in different cultures and at particular moments, for example in orgiastic mystery, then in the Platonic *anabasis*, then in the *mysterium tremendum*, apprehends death differently, giving itself each time a different approach. The approach or apprehension of death signifies the experience of anticipation while indissociably referring to the meaning of death that is suggested in this apprehensive approach. It is always a matter of seeing coming what one can't see coming, of giving oneself that which one can probably never give oneself in a pure and simple way. Each time the self anticipates death by giving to it or conferring upon it a different value, giving itself or reappropriating what in fact it cannot simply appropriate.

The first awakening to responsibility, in its Platonic form, corresponds, for Patočka, to a conversion with respect to the experience of death. Philosophy is born out of this form of responsibility, and in the same movement the philosopher is born to his own responsibility. It comes into being *as such* at the moment when the soul is not only gathering in the preparation for death but when it is ready to receive death, giving it to itself even, in an acceptation that delivers it from the body, and at the same time delivers it from the demonic and the orgiastic. By means of the passage to death the soul accedes to its own freedom.

But the *mysterium tremendum* announces, in a manner of speaking, *another death*; it announces another way of giving death or of granting oneself death. This time the word "gift" is uttered. This other way of apprehending death, and, there again, of acceding to responsibility, comes from a gift received from the other, from the one who, in absolute transcendence, sees me without my seeing, holds me in his hands while remaining inaccessible. The Christian "reversal" that converts the Platonic conversion *in turn*, involves the entrance upon the scene of a gift. An event gives the gift that transforms the Good into a Goodness forgetful of itself, into a love that renounces itself:

> Responsible life was itself presented as a *gift* of something which ultimately, though it has the character of the Good [that is, retaining, at the heart of the gift, the Platonic *agathon*], has also the traits of the inaccessible and forever superior to humans—the traits of the *mysterium* that always has the final word. (106, my italics)[1]

What is given—and this would also represent a kind of death—is not some thing, but goodness itself, a giving goodness, the act of giving or the donation of the gift. A goodness that must not only forget itself but whose source remains inaccessible to the donee. By means of this dissymmetry the donee receives what is also a death,

1. I have modified the English "a gift from something" in the light of Derrida's following comment.—Trans.

death given, the gift of dying in one way and not another. Above all it is a goodness whose inaccessibility acts as a command to the donee. It subjects its receivers, giving itself to them as goodness itself but also as the law. In order to understand in what way this gift of the law means not only the emergence of a new figure of responsibility but also of another kind of death, one has to take into account the uniqueness and irreplaceable singularity of the self as the means by which—and this is the approach to death—existence excludes every possible substitution. Now to have the experience of responsibility on the basis of the law that is given, to have the experience of one's absolute singularity and apprehend one's own death, amounts to the same thing. Death is very much that which nobody else can undergo or confront in my place. My irreplaceability is therefore conferred, delivered, "given," one can say, by death. It is the same gift, the same source, one could say the same goodness and the same law. It is from the perspective of death as the place of my irreplaceability, that is, of my singularity, that I feel called to responsibility. In this sense only a mortal can be responsible.

Once again, Patočka's gesture is, up to a certain point, comparable to Heidegger's. In *Being and Time*, the latter passes from a chapter where he was dealing with being-toward-death to a chapter on conscience (*Gewissen*), the call (*Ruf*), responsibility in the face of the call, and even responsibility as originary guilt (*Schuldigsein*). And he had indeed signaled that death is the place of one's irreplaceability. No one can die for me if "for me" means instead of me, in my place. "Der Tod ist, sofern er 'ist,' wesensmässig je der meine" ("By its very essence, death is in every case mine, in so far as it 'is' at all") (§47, 240 [284]).

This formulation was preceded by a consideration of sacrifice that basically foresees—exposing itself to it but exempting itself in advance—the objection that Lévinas constantly makes in relation to Heidegger, that, through the existence of the *Dasein*, he privileges "*my* [own] death."[2] Heidegger doesn't give any examples of sacrifice here, but one can imagine all sorts of them, in the public

---

2. Cf. Emmanuel Lévinas, *God, Death, and Time*, trans. Bettina Bergo (Stanford: Stanford University Press, 2000), 19 and passim.

space of religious or political communities, in the semiprivate space of families, in the secrecy of dual relations (dying for God, dying for the homeland, dying to save one's children or loved one). Giving one's life *for* the other, dying *for* the other, Heidegger insists, does not mean dying in the place of the other. On the contrary, it is only to the extent that dying—in so far as it "is"—remains mine, that I can die for another or *give* my life to the other. There is no gift of self, it cannot be thought, except in terms of this irreplaceability. Heidegger doesn't formulate it in those terms. However, it seems to me that one does not betray his thinking if one translates it in this way, for it has always, as much as has that of Lévinas, paid constant attention to the fundamental and founding possibility of sacrifice. Here again, after underlining the question of irreplaceability, Heidegger defines it as the condition of possibility of sacrifice, and not of its impossibility:

> No one can take the Other's dying away from him *(Keiner kann dem Anderen sein Sterben abnehmen)*. Of course someone can "go to his death for another" [this phrase is within quotation marks because of its almost proverbial character: to die for another *("für einen Anderen in den Tod gehen")*]. But that always means to sacrifice oneself for the Other *"in some definite affair" (für den Anderen sich opfern* "in einer bestimmten Sache"). (§47, 240 [284])

Heidegger underlines *in einer bestimmten Sache*, which means "for a determinate reason," from a particular and not a total point of view. I can give my whole life for another, I can offer my death to the other, but in doing so I will only be replacing or saving something partial in a particular situation (there will be a nonexhaustive exchange or sacrifice, an economy of sacrifice). I will not be dying *in place of the other*. I know on absolute grounds and in an absolutely certain manner that I will never deliver the other from his death, from the death that affects the whole of his being. For these ideas concerning death are, as one well knows, motivated by Heidegger's analysis of what he calls the *Daseinsganzheit* (the totality of the *Dasein*). It is indeed a case of the extent to which giving "for" means giving *to* death. Death's dative (dying *for* the other, giving one's life *to* the other) does not signify a substitution (*for* is not *pro* in the sense of "in place of the other"). If something radically impossible is to be conceived of—and everything derives its sense from this impossibility—it is indeed dying *for the other* in the sense of dying *in place of* the other. I can give the other everything except immortality, except this *dying for her* to the extent of dying in place of her, so freeing her from her own death. I can die for the other in a situation where my death gives him a little longer to live; I can save someone by throwing myself in the water or fire in order to snatch him temporarily from the jaws of death; I can give her my heart in the literal or figurative sense in order to assure her of a certain longevity. But I cannot die in her place, I cannot give her my life in exchange for her death. Only a mortal can give, as we said earlier. That should now be adjusted to read: and that mortal can give only to what is mortal, since he can give everything except immortality, everything except salvation as immortality. In that respect we obviously remain within Heidegger's logic of sacrifice, a logic that is, perhaps, neither that of Patočka, even if the latter seems to follow it up to this point, nor that of Lévinas.

But the arguments intersect in spite of their differences. They ground responsibility, as experience of singularity, in this apprehensive approach to death. The sense of responsibility is in all cases defined as a mode of "giving oneself death." Once it is established that I cannot die *for* another (in his place) although I can die *for* him (by sacrificing myself for him or dying before his eyes), my own death becomes this irreplaceability that I must assume if I wish to arrive at what is absolutely mine. My first and last responsibility, my first and last desire, is the responsibility of responsibility that relates me to what no one else can do in my place. It is thus also the very context of the *Eigentlichkeit* that, by caring, authentically relates me to my own possibility as possibility and freedom of the *Dasein*. The literality of this theme that is essential to *Being and Time* can be understood in its strictest sense as the irreplaceability of death:

> Such dying for (*Solches Sterben für*) can never signify that the Other has thus had his death taken away in even the slightest degree (*dem Anderen . . . abgenommen sei*). (ibid.)

This *abnehmen* (take away, remove from) receives a response, in the next sentence, from an *aufnehmen*, another form of taking, taking something upon oneself, assuming, accepting. Because I cannot take death away from the other who can no more take it from me in return, it remains for everyone to take his own death *upon himself*. Everyone must assume their own death, that is to say, the one thing in the world that no one else can *either give or take*: therein resides freedom and responsibility. For one could say, in French, at least in terms of this logic, that no one can either give me death or take it from me [*personne ne peut ni me donner la mort ni me prendre la mort*]. Even if one gives me death to the extent that it means killing me, that death will still have been mine, and as long as it is irreducibly mine I will not have received it from anyone else. Thus dying can never be borne, borrowed, transferred, delivered, promised, or transmitted. And just as it can't be given to me, so it can't be taken away from me. Death would be this possibility of *giving and taking* [*donner-prendre*] that actually exempts itself from the same realm of possibility that it institutes, namely from *giving and taking*. Death would be the name of whatever suspends every experience of *giving and taking*. But to say that is far from excluding the fact that it is only on the basis of death, and in its name, that *giving* and *taking* become possible.

The ideas that lead us to these last propositions, which figure literally neither in Patočka nor in Lévinas nor in Heidegger, derive from the latter's shift from *abnehmen* to *aufnehmen* in the sense of *auf sich nehmen* (to take upon oneself). The death that one cannot *abnehmen* (which one cannot take from another to spare him it, no more than he can take it from me or take mine), such a death void of any possible substitution, the death that one can take neither from the other nor to the other, must be taken upon oneself (*auf sich nehmen*). Heidegger says just prior to that that the death that "dying for" signifies in no way means that death can be *abgenommen*, spared the other. In plain terms: "Dying is something that every Dasein itself must take upon itself at the time" ("Das Sterben muss jedes Dasein jeweilig selbst auf sich nehmen") (ibid.).

In order to put oneself to death, to give oneself death in the sense that every relation to death is an interpretative apprehension and a representative approach to death, one must take death upon oneself. One has to *give it to oneself by taking it upon oneself*, for it can only be mine alone [*en propre*], irreplaceably. That is so even if, as we were just saying, *death can neither be taken nor given*. But the idea of being neither taken nor given relates *from* or *to* the other, and that is indeed why one can give it *to oneself* only by taking it *upon oneself*.

The question becomes concentrated in this "oneself," in the sameness [*le même*] or oneself [*le soi-même*] of the mortal or dying self. "Who" or "what" gives itself death or takes it upon him-, her- or itself? Let us note in passing that in none of these discourses that we are analyzing here does the moment of death give room for taking into account or marking sexual difference; as if, as it would be tempting to imagine, sexual difference no longer counts in the face of death. That would be the ultimate horizon, namely the end of sexual difference; sexual difference would be a being-*up-until-*death.

The sameness of one's self [*le même du soi-même*], what remains irreplaceable in dying, doesn't become what it is—in the sense of a same that relates to self in the oneself—before encountering what relates it to its mortality understood as irreplaceability. In the logic that Heidegger develops it is not a matter of oneself—a *Dasein* that cares—apprehending its *Jemeinigkeit* and so coming to be a being-toward-death. It is in the being-toward-death that the oneself of the *Jemeinigkeit* is constituted, comes into its own, that is, comes to realize its unsubstitutability. The sameness of the oneself is *given* by death, by the being-toward-death that *promises* me to it. It is only to the extent that this sameness of the oneself is posited as irreducibly different singularity that death for the other or the death of the other can make sense. Such an idea, in any case, never alters the oneself of the being-toward-death in the irreplaceability of the *Je-meinigkeit*; in fact it confirms it. To the extent that the mortal oneself of the *Jemeinigkeit* is originary and "nonderivable," it is indeed the place in which the call (*Ruf*) is heard and in which responsibility comes into play. In fact the *Dasein* must in the first instance answer for itself in the sameness of itself, receiving the call from nowhere other than itself. However, that doesn't prevent the *Dasein* from falling upon it: it falls *upon* it as though *from inside* itself, it imposes the call upon itself autonomously. Such is the basis for autonomy in the Kantian sense, for example: "The call comes *from* me and yet *from beyond me and over me*" ("*Der Ruf kommt* aus *mir und doch* über mich") (§57, 275 [320]).

One could find here the principle involved in Lévinas's objection to Heidegger (we will need to come back to it later in rereading Heidegger's analysis of death as possibility of the impossibility of the *Dasein*). Lévinas wants to remind us that responsibility is not at first responsibility of myself for myself, that the sameness of myself is derived from the perspective of the other, as if it were second to the other, coming to itself as responsible and mortal from the position of my responsibility before the other, for the other's death and in the face of it. In the first place it is because the *other* is mortal that my responsibility is singular and "inalienable":

> It is for the death of the other that I am responsible to the point of including myself in his death. This is perhaps shown in a more acceptable proposition: "I am responsible for the other in that he is mortal." The death of the other: therein lies the foremost death. (*God, Death and Time*, 43, translation modified)

What inclusion is being talked about here? How can one be included in another's death? How can one not be? What can be meant by "including myself in his death?" Until we are able to displace the logic or topology that prevents *good sense* from thinking that or "living" it, we will have no hope of coming close to Lévinas's thinking, nor of understanding what death teaches us [*nous ap-prend*], or gives us to think beyond the giving and taking [*donner-prendre*], in the *adieu*. What is the *adieu*? What does *adieu* mean? What does it mean to say "adieu?" How does one say and hear "*adieu*"? Not the *adieu* but *adieu*? And how can we think of death starting from *adieu* rather than the inverse?

We cannot effect such a displacement here. Let us remember, however, that Lévinas defines the first phenomenon of death as "responselessness" in a passage in which he declares that "intentionality is not the secret of the human" (so many paradoxical and provocative traits appear on the way to recalling the origin of responsibility): "The human *esse*, or existing, is not a *conatus* but disinterestedness and *adieu*" (*God, Death, and Time*, 15).

It seems to me that *adieu* can mean at least three things:

1. The salutation or benediction given (before all constative language, "adieu" can just as well signify "hello," "I can see you," "I see that you are there," I speak to you before telling you anything else—and in certain circumstances in French it happens that one says *adieu* at the moment of meeting rather than separation);

2. The salutation or benediction given at the moment of separation, of departure, sometimes forever (that can never in fact be excluded), without any return on this earth, at the moment of death;

3. The *à-dieu*, for God or before God and before anything else and in every relation to the other, in a wholly other adieu. Every relation to the other would be, before and after anything else, an adieu.

We can only glimpse here how this thought of the adieu (of "adieu") also challenges the primordial and ultimate character of the question of being or of the nonindifference of the *Dasein* with respect to its own being. Lévinas reproaches Heidegger not only because the *Dasein* is argued from the privileged position of its own death but because it gives itself death as a simple annihilation, a passage to nonbeing, which amounts to inscribing the death that is given, as being-toward-death, within the horizon of the question of being (*God, Death, and Time*, 50–51). On the other hand, the death of the other—or for the other—that which institutes our self and our responsibility, would correspond to a more originary experience than the comprehension or precomprehension of the sense of being: "The relation with death, more ancient than any experience, is not the vision of being or nothingness" (ibid., 15).

What is most ancient would here be the other, the possibility of dying *of* the other or *for* the other. Such a death is not given in the first instance as annihilation. It institutes responsibility as giving oneself death, *putting oneself to death* or *offering one's death*, that is to say *one's life*, in the ethical dimension of sacrifice.

Patočka is close to both Heidegger, whom he knew well, and Lévinas, whom he may or may not have read, but what he says differs from one and the other. Even if it sometimes seems slight or secondary, the difference does not reduce to one of intonation or pathos. It can also seem quite decisive. It is not only Patočka's Christianity that separates him from both of those two thinkers (for argument's sake, let us adopt the hypothesis that in what is most important to their thinking, Heidegger and Lévinas are not Christian, something that is far from being clear). Along with Christianity there is a certain idea of Europe, its history and future, that also distinguishes him from them. And since Patočka's Christian politics retains something heretical about it, one might even say a decided predisposition toward a certain principle of heresy, the situation is very complicated, not to say equivocal, which makes it all the more interesting.

Let us return to those intersections of agreement and disagreement that, up to this point, have been identified in Heidegger's and Lévinas's analyses of the "gift of death" as they refer to responsibility. In Patočka we could find all the same elements but in an overdetermined form, and thus radically transformed by his reference to a network of themes from Christianity.

The fact that Christian themes are identifiable does not mean that this text is, down to the last word and in its final signature, an essentially Christian one, even if Patočka could himself be said to be. It matters little in the end. Given that the essay involves a genealogy of European responsibility or of responsibility as Europe, of *Europe-responsibility* through the decoding of a certain history of mysteries, of their incorporation and their repression, it will always be possible to say that Patočka's text analyzes, deciphers, reconstitutes, or even deconstructs the history of this responsibility inasmuch as the latter transits through a certain history of Christianity (and who could say otherwise?). Moreover, the alternative between these two hypotheses (Christian text or not, Patočka as Christian thinker or not) is of limited pertinence. If it does involve Christianity, it is at the same time a heretical and hyperbolic version thereof. Patočka speaks and thinks in the places where Christianity has not yet thought or spoken of what it should have been and is not yet.

The Christian themes can be seen to revolve around the *gift* as gift of death, the fathomless gift of a type of death: infinite love (the

Good as goodness that infinitely forgets itself), sin and salvation, repentance and sacrifice. What engenders all these meanings and links them, internally and necessarily, is a logic that at bottom (and that is why it can still, up to a certain point, be called a "logic") has no need of *the event of a revelation or the revelation of an event*. It needs to think the possibility of such an event but not the event itself. This is a major point of difference, permitting such a discourse to be developed without reference to religion as institutional dogma, and proposing a thought-provoking genealogy of the possibility and essence of the religious that doesn't amount to an article of faith. If one takes into account certain differences, the same can be said for many discourses that seek in our day to be religious—discourses of a philosophical type if not philosophies themselves—without putting forth theses or theologems that would, by their very structure, teach something corresponding to the dogmas of a given religion. The difference is subtle and unstable, and it would require careful and vigilant analysis. In different respects and in different directions, the discourses of Lévinas or Jean-Luc Marion, perhaps of Ricoeur also, are in the same situation as that of Patočka. But in the final analysis this list has no clear limit and it can be said, once again taking into account the many differences, that a certain Kant and a certain Hegel, Kierkegaard of course—and I might even dare to say for provocative effect, Heidegger also—belong to this tradition that consists in proposing a nondogmatic doublet of dogma, a philosophical and metaphysical doublet, in any case a *thinking* that "repeats" the *possibility* of religion without religion. (We will need to return to this immense and thorny question elsewhere.)

How does this somewhat logical and philosophical deduction operate vis-à-vis the religious themes we have just mentioned (the gift of the Good as Goodness that is forgetful of itself, therefore the Good as infinite love, the gift of death, sin, repentance, sacrifice, salvation, etc.)? How does such thinking elaborate, in the style of a genealogy, a reply to the question concerning what conditions render responsibility possible? The response involves [*passe*] the logical necessity of a *possibility* for the event. Everything *comes to pass* as though only the analysis of the concept of responsibility were ultimately capable of producing Christianity, or more precisely the possibility of Christianity. One might as well conclude, conversely, that this concept of responsibility is Christian through and through and is produced by the event of Christianity. For if simply as a result of examining this concept the Christian event (sin, gift of infinite love linked to the experience of death), and it alone, appears necessary, does that not mean that Christianity alone has made possible access to an authentic responsibility throughout history, responsibility *as history* and as history of *Europe?* There is no choice to be made here between on the one hand a logical deduction, or one that is not related to the event, and the reference to a revelatory event. One implies the other. And it is not simply as a believer or as a Christian affirming dogma, the revelation, and the event, that Patočka makes the declaration already referred to, as would a genealogist historian stating what point history has arrived at:

> By virtue of this foundation in the abyssal deepening of the soul, Christianity remains thus far the greatest, unsurpassed but also un-thought-through human outreach that enabled humans to struggle against decadence. (108)

On what condition is responsibility possible? On the condition that the Good no longer be a transcendental objective, a relation between objective things, but the relation to the other, a response to the other; an experience of personal goodness, and a movement of intention. That supposes, as we have seen, a double rupture: *both* with orgiastic mystery *and* with Platonism. On what condition does goodness exist beyond all calculation? On the condition that goodness forget itself, that the movement is a movement of the gift that renounces itself, hence a movement of infinite love. Only infinite love can renounce itself and, in order to *become finite*, become incarnated in order to love the other, to love the other as a finite other. This gift of infinite love comes from someone and is addressed to someone; responsibility demands irreplaceable singularity. Yet only death, or rather the apprehension of death, can give this irreplaceability, and it is only on the basis of it that one can speak of a responsible subject, of the soul as conscience of self, of myself, etc. We have thus deduced the possibility of a mortal's accession to responsibility through the experience of his irreplaceability, that which an approaching death or the approach to death gives him. But the mortal thus deduced is someone whose very responsibility requires that she concern herself not only with an objective Good but with a gift of infinite love, a goodness that is forgetful of itself. There is thus a structural disproportion or dissymmetry between the finite and responsible mortal on the one hand and the goodness of the infinite gift on the other. One can think this disproportion without assigning to it a revealed cause or without tracing it back to the event of original sin, but it inevitably transforms the experience of responsibility into one of guilt: I have never been and never will be up to the level of this infinite goodness nor up to the immensity of the gift, the frameless immensity that must in general define (*in*-define) a gift as such. This guilt is originary, like original sin. Before any fault is determined I am guilty inasmuch as I am responsible. What gives me my singularity, namely death and finitude, is precisely what makes me unequal to the infinite goodness of the gift, which is also the first appeal to responsibility. Guilt is inherent in responsibility because responsibility is always unequal to itself: one is never responsible enough. One is never responsible enough because one is finite, but also because responsibility requires two contradictory movements. It requires one to respond as oneself and as irreplaceable singularity, to answer for what one does, says, gives; but it also requires that, being good and through goodness, one forget or efface the origin of what one gives. Patočka doesn't say that in so many words, and I am stretching things a little further than he or the letter of his text would allow. But it is he who deduces guilt and sin—and so repentance, sacrifice, and the seeking of salvation—in the situation of the responsible individual:

> The responsible human as such is *I*; it is an individual that is not identical with any role it could possibly assume [an interior and invisible self, a secret self at bottom]—in Plato this is expressed in the myth of the drawing of life's lot [a *pre*-Christian myth then, one that prepares for Christianity]; it is a responsible I because in the confrontation with death and in coming to terms with nothingness [a more "Heideggerian" than "Lévinasian" theme] it takes upon it-

self what we all must carry out in ourselves, where no one can take our place. Now, however, individuality is vested in a relation to an infinite love and humans are individuals because they are guilty, and *always* guilty, with respect to it. [Patočka underlines "always": like Heidegger he defines there an originary guilt that doesn't even wait for one to commit any particular fault, crime, or sin, an *a priori* guilt that is included in the conception of responsibility, in the originary *Schuldigsein*, which one can translate as "responsibility" as well as "guilt." But Heidegger has no need to make reference, no explicit reference at least, to this disproportion with respect to an infinite love in order to analyze the originary *Schuldigsein*.] We all, as individuals, are defined by the uniqueness of our individual placement in the universality of sin. (107)

THREE

Whom to Give to (Knowing Not to Know)

Mysterium tremendum. A frightful mystery, a secret to make you tremble.

Tremble. What does one do when one trembles? What is it that makes you tremble?

A secret always *makes* you tremble. Not simply quiver or shiver, which also happens sometimes, but tremble. A quiver can of course manifest fear, anguish, apprehension of death; as when one quivers in advance, in anticipation of what is to come. But it can be slight, on the surface of the skin, like when it announces the arrival of pleasure or an orgasm. It is a moment in passing, the suspended time of seduction. A quiver is not always very serious; it is sometimes discreet, barely discernible, somewhat epiphenomenal. It prepares for, rather than follows the event. One could say that water quivers before it boils; that is the idea I was referring to as seduction: a superficial pre-boil, a preliminary and visible agitation.

On the other hand, trembling, at least as a signal or symptom, is something that has already taken place, as in the case of an earthquake [*tremblement de terre*] or when one trembles all over. It is no longer preliminary even if, unsettling everything so as to imprint upon the body an irrepressible shaking, the event that makes one tremble portends and threatens still. It suggests that violence

is going to break out again, that some trauma will insist on being repeated. As different as dread, fear, anxiety, terror, panic, or
anguish remain from one another, they have already begun in the
trembling, and what has provoked them continues, or threatens to
continue to make us tremble. Most often we neither know nor see
the origin—secret, therefore—of what is coming upon us. We are
afraid of the fear, we anguish over the anguish, and we tremble.
We tremble in the strange repetition that ties an irrefutable past
(a shock has been felt, some trauma has already affected us) to a
future that cannot be anticipated; anticipated but unpredictable;
apprehended, yet, and this is why there is a future, apprehended
precisely *as* unforeseeable, unpredictable; approached *as* unap-
proachable. Even if one thinks one knows what is going to happen, the new instant, the arriving [*arrivant*] of that arrival remains
untouched, still inaccessible, in fact unlivable. In the repetition of
what still remains unpredictable, we tremble first of all because
we don't know from which direction the shock came, whence it
was given (whether a good surprise or a bad shock, sometimes a
surprise received *as* a shock); and we tremble from not knowing,
in the form of a double secret, whether it is going to continue,
start again, insist, be repeated: whether it will, how it will, where,
when; and why this shock. Hence I tremble because I am still
afraid of what already makes me afraid and which I can neither
see nor foresee. I tremble before what exceeds my seeing and my
knowing [*mon voir et mon savoir*] although it concerns the inner-
most parts of me, right down to my soul, down to the bone, as we
say. Inasmuch as it tends to undo both seeing and knowing, trembling is indeed an experience of secrecy or of mystery, but another
secret, another enigma, or another mystery comes to overlay the
unlivable experience, adding yet another seal or concealment to
the *tremor*. (That is the Latin word for "trembling," from *tremo*,
which in Greek as in Latin means *I tremble, I am afflicted by trembling*; in Greek there is also *tromeō*: I tremble, I shiver, I am afraid;
and *tromos*, which means trembling, fear, fright. In Latin, *tremen-
dus, tremendum*, as in *mysterium tremendum*, is a gerundive derived
from *tremo*: what makes one tremble, something frightening, dis-
tressing, terrifying.)

Where does this supplementary seal come from? One doesn't know *why one trembles*. This limit to knowledge no longer relates only to the cause or event, the unfamiliar, unseen, or unknown that makes us tremble. Neither do we know why it produces this particular symptom, a certain irrepressible agitation of the body, the uncontrollable instability of its members, a tremor of the skin or muscles. Why does the irrepressible take this form? Why does terror make us tremble, since one can also tremble with cold, and such analogous physiological manifestations translate experiences and sentiments that appear, at least, not to have anything in common? This symptomatology is as enigmatic as that of tears. Even if one knows why one weeps, in what situation and what it signifies (I weep because I have lost one of my nearest and dearest, the child cries because he has been beaten or because she is not loved: she causes herself grief, complains, he makes himself complain or allows himself to be felt sorry for—by means of the other), but that still doesn't explain why the lachrymal glands come to secrete these drops of water which are brought to the eyes rather than elsewhere, the mouth or the ears. We would need to make new inroads into the thinking of the body, without dissociating the registers of discourse (thought, philosophy, the bio-genetico-psychoanalytic sciences, phylo- and ontogenesis), in order to one day come closer to what makes us tremble or what makes us cry, to that *cause* which is not the final cause that can be called God or death (God is the cause of the *mysterium tremendum*, and the death that is given is always what makes us tremble, or what makes us weep as well) but the closest cause; not the immediate cause, that is to say the accident or circumstance, but the cause closest to our body, that which brings about trembling or weeping rather than something else. What are they metaphors or figures for? What does *the body mean* (*to say*) by trembling or crying, presuming one can speak here of the body, of saying or meaning, and of rhetoric?

What makes us tremble in the *mysterium tremendum*? It is the gift of infinite love, the dissymmetry that exists between the divine regard that sees me, and myself, who doesn't see what is looking at me; it is the gift and endurance of death that exists in the irreplaceable, the disproportion between the infinite gift and my finitude, responsibility as culpability, sin, salvation, repentance, and sacrifice. As in the title of Kierkegaard's essay *Fear and Trembling*,[1] the *mysterium tremendum* includes an at least implicit and indirect reference to Saint Paul. In the Epistle to the Philippians 2:12, the disciples are asked to work toward their salvation in fear and trembling. They will have to work for their salvation knowing all along that it is God who decides: the Other has no reason to give to us and no explanation to make, no reason to share his reasons with us. We fear and tremble because we are already in the hands of God, although free to work, but in the hands and under the gaze of God, whom we don't see and whose will we cannot know, no more than the decisions he will hand down, nor his reasons for wanting this or that, our life or death, our salvation or perdition. We fear and tremble before the inaccessible secret of a God who decides for us although we remain responsible, that is to say free to decide, to work, to assume our life and our death.

So Paul says—and this is one of the "adieux" I mentioned earlier:

> Wherefore my beloved, as ye have always obeyed, not as in my presence only, but now much more in my absence (*non ut in praesentia mei tantum, sed multo magis nunc in absentia mea / mē hōs en tē parousia mou monon alla nun pollō mallon en tē apousia mou*), work out your own salvation with fear and trembling (*cum metu et tremore / meta phobou kai tromou*).[2]

This is a first explanation of the fear and of the trembling, and of "fear and trembling." The disciples are asked to work toward their salvation not in the presence (*parousia*) but in the absence (*apousia*) of the master: without either seeing or knowing, without hearing the law or the reasons for the law. Without knowing from whence the thing comes and what awaits us, we are given over to absolute solitude. No one can speak with us and no one can speak for us; we

---

1. Søren Kierkegaard, *Kierkegaard's Writings*, vol. 6, *Fear and Trembling, and Repetition*, ed. and trans. Howard V. Hong and Edna H. Hong (Princeton: Princeton University Press, 1983). Page references are to this edition.

2. Philippians 2:12. All biblical quotations are from the King James Version. —Trans.

must take it upon ourselves, each of us must take it upon himself (*auf sich nehmen*, as Heidegger was saying concerning death, our death, concerning what is always "my death," and which no one can take on in place of me). But there is something even more serious at the origin of this trembling. If Paul says "adieu" and absents himself as he asks them to obey, in fact ordering them to obey (for one doesn't ask for obedience, one orders it), it is because God is himself absent, hidden and silent, separate, secret, at the moment he has to be obeyed. God doesn't give his reasons, he acts as he intends, he doesn't have to give his reasons or share anything with us: neither his motivations, if he has any, nor his deliberations, nor even his decisions. Otherwise he wouldn't be God, we wouldn't be dealing with the Other as God or with God as *wholly other* [*tout autre*]. If the other were to share his reasons with us by explaining them to us, if he were to speak to us all the time without any secrets, he wouldn't be the other, we would share a type of homogeneity. Discourse also partakes of that sameness; we don't speak with God or to God, we don't speak with God or to God as with others or to our fellows. Paul continues in fact:

> For it is God which worketh in you both to will and to do of his good pleasure. (Philippians 2:13)[3]

One can understand why Kierkegaard chose, for his title, the words of a great Jewish convert, Paul, when it came to meditating on the still Jewish experience of a secret, hidden, separate, absent, or mysterious God, the one who decides, without revealing his reasons, to demand of Abraham that most cruel, impossible, and untenable

---

3. In sometimes adding the Greek or Latin, I am following the Grosjean and Léturmy translation (Bibliothèque de la Pléiade). What they translate as *son bon plaisir* ("his good pleasure") doesn't refer to God's pleasure but to his *sovereign* will that is not required to consult with anybody, just as the king acts as he pleases without revealing his secret reasons, without having to account for it or explain it. The text names not God's pleasure but his will: *pro bona voluntate* or *hyper tēs eudokias*. *Eudokia* means "good will," not just in the sense of a will that is good (desiring the good), but of a simple will that judges well, for its pleasure, as in their translation; for that is his will and it suffices. *Eudokeō*: "I judge well," "I approve," sometimes "I am pleased" or "I take pleasure in," "I consent."

gesture: to offer his son Isaac as a sacrifice. All that goes on in secret. God keeps silent about his reasons. Abraham does also, and
the book is not signed by Kierkegaard, but by Johannes de Silentio
("a poetic person who only exists among poets," Kierkegaard writes
in the margin of his text [Pap. IV B 79, *Fear and Trembling*, 243]).

This pseudonym keeps silent, it expresses the silence that is kept.
Like all pseudonyms, it seems destined to keep secret the real name
as patronym, namely the name of the father of the work, in fact the
name of the father of the father of the work. This pseudonym, one
among many that Kierkegaard employed, reminds us of something
obvious: a meditation linking the question of secrecy to that of responsibility immediately addresses the name and the signature. One
often thinks that responsibility consists in acting and signing *in one's
name*. A responsible reflection on responsibility is interested in advance in whatever happens to the name in the event of pseudonym-
ity, metonymy, homonymy, in the question of what constitutes *a
real name*. Sometimes one says or wishes it more effectively, more
authentically, in the secret name by which *one calls oneself*, which *one
gives oneself or affects to give oneself*, the name that is more *naming* and
named in the pseudonym that in the official legality of the public
patronym.

The trembling of *Fear and Trembling*, is, or so it seems, the very
experience of sacrifice. Not, first of all, in the Hebraic sense of the
term, *korban*, which refers more to an approach or a "coming close
to," and which has been wrongly translated as "sacrifice," but inasmuch as sacrifice presumes the putting to death of the unique in
terms of its being unique, irreplaceable, and most precious. It also
therefore refers to the impossibility of substitution, the unsubstitut-
able; and then also to the substitution of an animal for man; and
finally, especially this, by means of this impossible substitution itself,
it refers to what links the sacred to sacrifice and sacrifice to secrecy.

Kierkegaard–de Silentio recalls Abraham's strange reply to Isaac
when the latter asks him where the lamb is to be found for the
sacrifice. It can't be said that Abraham doesn't respond to him. He
says God will provide. God will provide a lamb for the holocaust
(["burnt offering,"] Genesis 22:8). Abraham thus keeps his secret at
the same time as he replies to Isaac. He doesn't keep silent and he

doesn't lie. He doesn't speak nontruth. In *Fear and Trembling* (*Problema III*), Kierkegaard reflects on this double secret: between God and Abraham but also between the latter and his family. Abraham doesn't speak of what God has ordered him, and him alone, to do, he doesn't speak of it to Sarah, or to Eliezer, or to Isaac. He must keep the secret (that is his duty), but it is also a secret which he *must* keep as a double necessity because at bottom he *can only* keep it: he doesn't know it, he is unaware of its ultimate rhyme and reason. He is sworn to secrecy because he is in secret.

Because, in this way, he doesn't speak, Abraham transgresses the ethical order. According to Kierkegaard, the highest expression of the ethical is in terms of what binds us to our own and to our fellows (that can be the family but also the actual community of friends or the nation). By keeping the secret, Abraham betrays ethics. His silence, or at least the fact that he doesn't divulge the secret of the sacrifice he has been asked to make, is certainly not designed to save Isaac.

Of course, in some respects Abraham does speak. He says a lot. But even if he says everything, he need only keep silent on one single thing for it to be concluded that he hasn't spoken. Such a silence takes over his whole discourse. So he speaks and doesn't speak. He responds without responding. He responds and doesn't respond. He responds indirectly. He speaks in order not to say anything about the essential thing that he must keep secret. Speaking in order not to say anything is always the best technique for keeping a secret. Still, Abraham doesn't just speak in order not to say anything when he replies to Isaac. He says something that is not nothing and that is not false. He says something that is not a nontruth, something moreover that, although *he doesn't know it yet*, will turn out to be true.

To the extent that, in not saying the essential thing, namely the secret between God and him, Abraham doesn't speak, he assumes the responsibility that consists in always being alone, retrenched in one's own singularity at the moment of decision. Just as no one can die in my place, no one can make a decision, what we call "a decision," in my place. But as soon as one speaks, as soon as one enters the medium of language, one loses that very singularity. One therefore loses the possibility or the right to decide. Thus every decision would, fundamentally, remain at the same time solitary, secret, and silent. Speaking relieves us, Kierkegaard notes, for it "translates" into the general (113).[4]

The first effect or first destination of language therefore deprives me of, or delivers me from, my singularity. By suspending my absolute singularity in speaking, I renounce at the same time my liberty and my responsibility. Once I speak, I am never and no longer myself, alone and unique. This is such a strange contract—both paradoxical and terrifying—that binds infinite responsibility to silence and secret. It goes against what one usually thinks, even in the most philosophical mode. For common sense, just as for philosophical reasoning, the most widely shared presumption is that responsibility is tied to the public and to the nonsecret, to the possibility and even the necessity of accounting for one's words and actions in front of others, of justifying and owning up to them. Here, on the contrary, it appears just as necessarily that the absolute responsibility of my actions, to the extent that it has to remain mine, singularly so, something no one else can perform in my place, implies instead secrecy. But what is also implied is that, by not speaking to others, I don't account for my actions, I answer for nothing, I make no response to others or before others. It is both a scandal and a paradox. According to Kierkegaard, *ethical* exigency is regulated by the generality; and it therefore defines a responsibility that consists of *speaking*, that is to say of involving oneself sufficiently in the generality to justify oneself, to give an account of one's decision and to answer for one's actions. On the other hand, what does Abraham teach us, in his approach to sacrifice? That far from ensuring responsibility, the generality of ethics incites to irresponsibility. It impels me to speak, to reply, to account for, and thus to dissolve my singularity in the medium of the concept.

4. The English translation gives "the universal" for *det Almene*, whereas "the general" is closer to the Danish and is the term Derrida uses. Note also Kierkegaard's distinction between *individuel* ("individual") and *enkelt* ("singular"), which anticipates Derrida's here. For this and other clarifications of the English translation I am grateful to Elsebet Jegstrup and Mark Taylor.—Trans.

Such is the aporia of responsibility: one always risks not managing to accede to the concept of responsibility in the process of *forming* it. For responsibility (we would no longer dare speak of "the universal concept of responsibility") demands on the one hand an accounting, a general answering-for-oneself with respect to the general and before the generality, hence the idea of substitution; and on the other hand, uniqueness, absolute singularity, hence nonsubstitution, nonrepetition, silence, and secrecy. What I am saying here about responsibility can also be said about decision. The ethical involves me in substitution, as does speaking. Whence the insolence of the paradox: for Abraham, Kierkegaard declares, *the ethical is a temptation*. He must therefore resist it. He keeps silent in order to escape the moral temptation which, under the pretext of calling him to responsibility, to self-justification, would make him lose his ultimate responsibility along with his singularity, make him lose his unjustifiable, secret, and absolute responsibility before God. This is ethics as "irresponsibilization," as an insoluble and therefore paradoxical contradiction between responsibility *in general* and *absolute* responsibility. Absolute responsibility is not a responsibility, at least it is not general responsibility or responsibility in general. It needs to be exceptional or extraordinary, and it needs to be that absolutely and par excellence: it is as if absolute responsibility could no longer be derived from a *concept* of responsibility, and therefore, in order for it to be what it must be, it must remain inconceivable, indeed unthinkable: it must therefore be irresponsible in order to be absolutely responsible. "Abraham *cannot* speak, because he cannot say that which would explain everything . . . that it is an ordeal such that, please note, the ethical is the temptation" (115).

The ethical can therefore end up making us irresponsible. It is a temptation, a tendency or a facility that would sometimes have to be refused in the name of a responsibility that doesn't calculate or give an account, neither to man, to humans, to society, to our fellows, or to our own. Such a responsibility keeps its secret, it cannot and need not present itself. Tyrannically, jealously, it refuses to present itself before the violence that consists of asking for accounts and justifications, summonses to appear before the law of men. It declines the autobiography that is always auto-justification, *égodicée*.

Abraham *presents himself*, of course, but before God, the unique, jealous, secret God, the one to whom he says "Here I am." But in order to do that, he must renounce his family loyalties, which amounts to violating his oath, and refuse to present himself before men. He no longer speaks to them. That at least is what the sacrifice of Isaac suggests (it would be different for a tragic hero such as Agamemnon).

In the end secrecy is as intolerable for ethics as it is for philosophy or for dialectics in general, from Plato to Hegel:

> The ethical as such is the universal; as the universal it is in turn the disclosed. The single individual, qualified as immediate, sensate, and psychical, is the hidden. Thus his ethical task is to work himself out of his hiddenness and to become disclosed in the universal. Every time he desires to remain in the hidden, he trespasses and is immersed in spiritual trial from which he can emerge only by disclosing himself.
>
> Once again we stand at the same point. If there is no hiddenness rooted in the fact that the single individual as the single individual is higher than the universal, then Abraham's conduct cannot be defended, for he disregarded the intermediary ethical categories. But if there is such a hiddenness, then we face the paradox, which does not allow itself to be mediated, since it is based precisely on this: the single individual as the single individual is higher than the universal. . . . The Hegelian philosophy assumes no justified hiddenness, no justified incommensurability. It is, then, consistent for it to demand disclosure, but it is a little bemuddled when it wants to regard Abraham as the father of faith and to speak about faith. (82, translation modified)

In the exemplary form of its absolute coherence, Hegel's philosophy represents the irrefutable demand for manifestation, phenomenalization, and unveiling; thus, it is thought, it represents the request for truth that inspires philosophy and ethics in their most powerful forms. There are no final secrets for philosophy, ethics, or politics. The manifest is given priority over the secret; universal generality is superior to individual singularity; no irreducible secret can be legally justified (*fondé en droit* says the French translation)—and hence the instance of the law has to be added to those of philosophy and ethics; there is no absolutely legitimate secret. But the paradox of faith is that interiority remains "incommensurable with exteriority" (69). No manifestation can consist in rendering the interior exterior or in showing what is hidden. The knight of faith can neither communicate to nor be understood by anyone, she can't help the other at all (71). The absolute duty that obligates her with respect to God cannot have the form of generality that is called duty. If I obey in my duty toward God (which is my absolute duty) *in terms of duty alone*, I am not entering into a relation with God. In order to fulfill my duty toward God himself, I must not act *out of duty*, by means of that form of generality called duty, which can always be mediated and communicated. The absolute duty that binds me to God himself, in faith, must function beyond and against all duty: "The duty becomes duty by being traced back to God, but in the duty itself I do not enter into relation to God" (68). Kant explains that to act morally is to act "out of duty" and not only "by conforming to duty." Kierkegaard sees acting "out of duty," in the universalizable sense of the law, as a dereliction of one's absolute duty. It is in this sense that absolute duty (toward God and in the singularity of faith) implies a sort of gift or sacrifice that reaches toward a faith beyond both debt and duty, beyond duty as a form of debt. This is the dimension that provides for a "gift of death" which, beyond human responsibility, beyond the universal concept of duty, is a response to absolute duty.

In the order of human generality, a duty of hate is implied. Kierkegaard quotes Luke 14:26: "'If any one comes to me and does not hate his own father and mother and his wife and children and brothers and sisters, yes, and even his own life, he cannot be my disciple.'" Recognizing that "this is a hard saying" (72), Kierkegaard nevertheless upholds the necessity of it. He refines its rigor without seeking to make it less shocking or paradoxical. But Abraham's hatred for the ethical and thus for his own (family, friends, relatives, nation, but at the outside humanity as a whole, his own kind or species) must remain an absolute source of pain. If I put to death or grant death to what I hate, it is not a sacrifice. I must sacrifice what I love. I must come to hate what I love, in the same moment, at the instant of granting death. I must hate and betray my own, that is to say offer them the gift of death by means of the sacrifice, not insofar as I hate them—that would be too easy—but insofar as I love them. I must hate them insofar as I love them. Hate wouldn't be hate if it hated only the hateful, that would be too easy. It must hate and betray what is most lovable. Hate cannot be hate, it can only be the sacrifice of love to love. It is not a matter of hating, of betraying by a breach of trust, or of offering the gift of death to what one doesn't love.

But is this heretical or paradoxical knight of faith Jewish, Christian, or Judeo-Christian-Islamic? The sacrifice of Isaac belongs to what one might just dare to call the common treasury, the terrifying secret of the *mysterium tremendum* that is a property of all three so-called religions of the Book, the religions of the races of Abraham. This exaggerated rigor, and the demand it entails, compel the knight of faith to say and do things that will appear (and *must* even be) atrocious. They will necessarily revolt those who profess allegiance to morality in general, to Judeo-Christian-Islamic morality or to the religion of love in general. But as Patočka will say, perhaps Christianity has not yet thought through its own essence, any more than it has the irrefutable events out of which Judaism, Christianity, and Islam have emerged. One cannot ignore or erase the sacrifice of Isaac recounted in Genesis, nor that recounted by Luke in the Gospels. It has to be taken into account, which is what Kierkegaard proposes. Abraham comes to hate those closest to him by keeping silent, he comes to hate his only beloved son by consenting to put him to death [*lui donner la mort*]. He hates them not out of hatred, of course, but out of love. He doesn't hate any less for all that, on the contrary. Abraham must love his son absolutely in order to come to the point where he will grant him death, to commit what ethics would call hatred and murder.

How does one hate one's own? Kierkegaard rejects the common distinction between love and hate, he finds it egoistic and without interest. He reinterprets it as a paradox. God wouldn't have asked Abraham to put Isaac to death, that is to say to make a gift of death

as a sacrificial offering to himself, to God, unless Abraham's love
for his son was absolute, unique, and incommensurable:

> for it is indeed this love for Isaac that makes his act a sacri-
> fice by its paradoxical contrast to his love for God. But the
> distress and the anxiety in the paradox is that he, humanly
> speaking, is thoroughly incapable of making himself un-
> derstandable. Only *in the instant* when his act is in absolute
> contradiction to his feelings, only then does he sacrifice
> Isaac, but the reality of his act is that by which he belongs
> to the universal, and there he is and remains a murderer.
> (74, translation modified)

I have underlined the word *instant*: "the instant of decision is madness," Kierkegaard says elsewhere. The paradox cannot be grasped
in time and through mediation, that is to say in language and
through reason. Like the gift and "the gift of death," it remains
irreducible to presence or to presentation, it demands a temporality of the instant without ever constituting a present. It belongs to
an atemporal temporality, to a duration that cannot be grasped:
something one can neither stabilize, establish, *grasp* [*prendre*], *apprehend*, or *comprehend*. Understanding, common sense, and reason
cannot seize, conceive, understand [*begreifen*], or mediate it; neither
can they negate or deny it, implicate it in the labor of the negative,
make it work: in the act of *giving death*, sacrifice suspends both the
labor of the negative and labor itself, perhaps even the work of
mourning. The tragic hero has access to mourning. Abraham, on
the other hand, is neither a man of mourning nor a tragic hero.

In order to assume his absolute responsibility vis-à-vis absolute
duty, to put his faith in God to work, or to the test, he must also in
reality remain a hateful murderer, for he consents to put to death.
In both general and abstract terms, the absoluteness of duty, of responsibility, and of obligation certainly demands that one transgress
ethical duty, although in betraying it one still belongs to it and at
the same time recognizes it. The contradiction and the paradox
must be endured *in the instant itself*. The two duties must contradict
one another, one must subordinate (incorporate, repress) the other.
Abraham must assume absolute responsibility for sacrificing his son

by sacrificing ethics, but in order for there to be a sacrifice, the ethical must retain all its value; the love for his son must remain intact, and the order of human duty must continue to insist on its rights.

The account of Isaac's sacrifice can be read as a narrative development of the paradox that inhabits the concept of duty or of absolute responsibility. This concept puts us into relation (but without relating to it, in a double secret) with the absolute other, with the absolute singularity of the other, whose name here is God. Whether or not one believes the biblical story, whatever credence or credit one gives to it, whether one doubts or transposes it, it could still be said that there is a moral to this story, even if we take it to be a fable (but taking it to be a fable still amounts to losing it to philosophical or poetic generality; it means that it loses the quality of an historic event). The moral of the fable would be morality itself, the point where morality brings into play the gift of the death that is so given. The absolutes of duty and of responsibility presume that one denounce, refute, and transcend, at the same time, all duty, all responsibility, and every human law. They call for a betrayal of everything that manifests itself within the order of universal generality, and everything that manifests itself in general, the very order and essence of manifestation; namely essence itself, essence in general to the extent that it is inseparable from presence and from manifestation. Absolute duty demands that one behave in an irresponsible manner (by means of treachery or betrayal), while still recognizing, confirming, and reaffirming the very thing one sacrifices, namely the order of human ethics and responsibility. In a word, ethics must be sacrificed in the name of duty. It is a duty not to respect, out of duty, ethical duty. One must behave not only in an ethical or responsible manner, but in a nonethical, nonresponsible manner, and one must do that *in the name of* duty, of an infinite duty, *in the name of* absolute duty. And this name, which must always be singular, is here none other than the name of God as wholly other, the nameless name of God, the unpronounceable name of God as other to which I am bound by an absolute, unconditional obligation, by an incomparable, nonnegotiable duty. The other as absolute other, namely God, must remain transcendent, hidden, secret, jealous of the love, requests, and commands that he gives and that he asks to be kept secret. Secrecy is essential to the exercise of this absolute responsibility as sacrificial responsibility.

In terms of the moral of morality, let us here insist upon what is too often forgotten by the moralizing moralists and good consciences who preach to us with assurance every morning and every week, in newspapers and magazines, on the radio and on television, about ethical or political responsibility. Philosophers who don't write ethics are failing in their duty, one often hears, and the first duty of the philosopher is to think about ethics, to add a chapter on ethics to each of his or her books and, in order to do that, to come back to Kant as often as possible. What the knights of good conscience don't realize, is that "the sacrifice of Isaac" illustrates—if that is the word in the case of such a nocturnal mystery—the most common and everyday experience of responsibility. The story is no doubt monstrous, outrageous, barely conceivable: a father is ready to put to death his beloved son, his irreplaceable loved one, and that because the Other, the great Other, asks him or orders him without giving the slightest explanation. An infanticide father who hides what he is going to do, without knowing why, from his son and from his family, what could be more abominable, what mystery could be more frightful (*tremendum*) vis-à-vis love, humanity, the family, or morality?

But isn't this also the most common thing? what the most cursory examination of the concept of responsibility cannot fail to affirm? Duty or responsibility binds me to the other, to the other as other, and binds me in my absolute singularity to the other as other. God is the name of the absolute other as other and as unique (the God of Abraham defined as the one and unique). As soon as I enter into a relation with the absolute other, my singularity enters into relation with his on the level of obligation and duty. I am responsible before the other as other; I answer to him and I answer for what I do before him. But of course, what binds me thus in my singularity to the absolute singularity of the other immediately propels me into the space or risk of absolute sacrifice. There are also others, an infinite number of them, the innumerable generality of others to whom I should be bound by the same responsibility, a general and universal responsibility (what Kierkegaard calls the ethical order).

I cannot respond to the call, the request, the obligation, or even the love of another without sacrificing the other other, the other others. *Every other (one) is every (bit) other* [*tout autre est tout autre*]; everyone else is completely or wholly other. The simple concepts of alterity and of singularity constitute the concept of duty as much as that of responsibility. As a result, the concepts of responsibility, of decision, or of duty, are condemned *a priori* to paradox, scandal, and aporia. Paradox, scandal, and aporia are themselves nothing other than sacrifice, the exposure of conceptual thinking to its limit, to its death and finitude. As soon as I enter into a relation with the other, with the gaze, look, request, love, command, or call of the other, I know that I can respond only by sacrificing ethics, that is to say by sacrificing whatever obliges me to also respond, in the same way, in the same instant, to all the others. I put to death, I betray and lie, I don't need to raise my knife over my son on Mount Moriah for that. Day and night, at every instant, on all the Mount Moriahs of this world, I am doing that, raising my knife over what I love and must love, over the other, to this or that other to whom I owe absolute fidelity, incommensurably. Abraham is faithful to God only in his treachery, in the betrayal of his own, and in the betrayal of the uniqueness of each one of them, exemplified here in his only beloved son. He would not be able to opt for fidelity to his own, or to his son, unless he were to betray the absolute other: God, if you wish.

Let us not look for examples, there would be too many of them, at every step we took. By preferring what I am doing here and now, simply by giving it my time and attention, by giving priority to my work or my activity as a citizen or professorial and professional philosopher, writing and speaking here in a public language, French in my case, I am perhaps fulfilling my duty. But I am sacrificing and betraying at every moment all my other obligations: my obligations to the other others whom I know or don't know, the billions of my fellows [*semblables*] (without mentioning the animals that are even more other than my fellows) who are dying of starvation or sickness. I betray my fidelity or my obligations to other citizens, to those who don't speak my language and to whom I neither speak nor respond, to each of those who listen or read, and to whom I neither respond nor address myself in the proper manner, that is to say in a singular manner (this for the so-called public space to which I sacrifice my so-called private space), thus also to those I love in private, my own, my family, my sons, each of whom is the only son I sacrifice to the other, every one being sacrificed to every one else in this land of Moriah that is our habitat every second of every day.

This is not just a figure of style or an effect of rhetoric. According to 2 Chronicles, chapters 3 and 8, the place where the sacrifice of Abraham or of Isaac (and it is the sacrifice of both of them, it is the gift of death one makes to the other in putting *oneself* to death, mortifying oneself in order to make a gift of this death as a sacrificial offering to God) is said to have occurred, this place where death is given or offered, is the place where Solomon decided to build the House of the Lord in Jerusalem, as well as the place where God appeared to Solomon's father, David. However, it is also the place of the grand Mosque of Jerusalem, the place called the Dome of the Rock near the grand mosque of El Aksa where the sacrifice of Ibrahim is supposed to have taken place, and from where Mahomet was transported on horseback toward paradise after his death. It is just above the destroyed temple of Jerusalem and the Wailing Wall, not far from the Way of the Cross. It is therefore a holy place but also a place that is in dispute, radically and rabidly, fought over by all the monotheisms, by all the religions of the unique and transcendent God, of the absolute other. These three monotheisms fight over it, it is useless to deny it by means of some wide-eyed ecumenism; they make war with fire and blood, have always done so and all the more fiercely today, each claiming its particular perspective on this place and claiming an original historical and political interpretation of Messianism and of the sacrifice of Isaac. The reading, interpretation, and tradition of the sacrifice of Isaac are themselves sites of bloody, holocaustic sacrifice. Isaac's sacrifice continues every day. Countless machines of death wage a war that has no front. There is no front between responsibility and irresponsibility but only between different appropriations of the same sacrifice, different orders of responsibility also, different other orders: the religious and the ethical, the religious and the ethico-political, the theological and the political, the theologico-political, the theocratic and the ethico-political, and so on; the secret and the public, the profane and the sacred, the specific and the generic, the human and the nonhuman. Sacrificial war rages not only among the religions of the Book and the races of Abraham that expressly refer to the sacrifice of Isaac, Ishmael, Abraham or Ibrahim, but between them and the rest of the starving world, within the immense majority of humankind and even those living (not to mention the others, dead or nonliving, dead or not yet born) who don't belong to the people of Abraham or Ibrahim, all those others to whom the names of Abraham and Ibrahim have never meant anything because they don't conform or correspond to anything.

I can respond to the one (or to the One), that is to say to the other, only by sacrificing to that one the other. I am responsible to any one (that is to say to the other) only by failing in my responsibilities to all the others, to the ethical or political generality. And I can never justify this sacrifice, I must always hold my peace about it. Whether I want to or not, I will never be able to justify the fact that I prefer or sacrifice any one (any other) to the other. I will always be in secret, held to secrecy in respect of this, for nothing can be said about it. What binds me to singularities, to this one or that one, male or female, rather than that one or this one, remains finally unjustifiable (this is Abraham's hyperethical sacrifice), as unjustifiable as the infinite sacrifice I make at each moment. These singularities represent others, a wholly other form of alterity: one other or some other persons, but also places, animals, languages. How would you ever justify the fact that you sacrifice all the cats in the world to the cat that you feed at home every day for years, whereas other cats die of hunger at every instant? Not to mention other people? How would you justify your presence here speaking one particular language, rather than there speaking to others in another language? And yet we also do our duty by behaving thus. There is no language, no reason, no generality or mediation to justify this ultimate responsibility which leads us to absolute sacrifice; absolute sacrifice that is not the sacrifice of irresponsibility on the altar of responsibility, but the sacrifice of the most imperative duty (that which binds me to the other as a singularity in general) in favor of another absolutely imperative duty binding me to the wholly other.

God decides to suspend the sacrificial process. He addresses Abraham, who has just said, "Here I am." "Here I am": the first and only possible response to the call by the other, the originary moment of responsibility such as it exposes me to the singular other, the one who appeals to me. "Here I am" is the only self-presentation presumed by every form of responsibility: I am ready to respond, I reply that I am ready to respond. Whereas Abraham has just said "Here I am," and taken his knife to slit his son's throat, God says to him, "Lay not thine hand upon the lad, neither do thou anything unto him: for now I know that thou fearest God, seeing thou hast not withheld thy son, thine only son, from me" (Genesis 22:12). This terrible declaration seems to display God's satisfaction at the terror that has been expressed (I see that "you fear God [*Elo-him*]," you tremble before me). It causes one to tremble through the fear and trembling it evokes as its only reason (I see that you have trembled before me, okay, we are quits, I free you from your obligation). But it can also be translated or argued as follows: I see that you have understood what absolute duty means, namely how to respond to the absolute other, to his call, request, or command. These different registers amount to the same thing: by command-ing Abraham to sacrifice his son, to put his son to death by offering a gift of death to God, by means of this double gift wherein the gift of death consists in putting to death by raising one's knife over someone and of putting death forward by giving it as an offering, God leaves him free to refuse—and that is the test. The command is requesting, like a prayer from God, a declaration of love that implores: tell me that you love me, tell me that you turn toward me, toward the unique one, toward the other as unique and, above all, over everything else, unconditionally; and in order to do that, make a gift of death, give death to your only son and give me the death I ask for, that I give to you by asking you for it. In short God says to Abraham: I can see right away [*à l'instant*] that you have understood what absolute duty toward the unique one means, that it means responding where there is no reason to be asked for or given; I see that not only have you understood that as an idea, but that—and here lies responsibility—you have acted on it, you have put it into effect, you were ready to carry it out *at this very instant* (God stops him *at the instant when there is no more time, where time is no more given*, as if Abraham had *already* killed Isaac: the concept of the instant is always indispensable): thus you had *already* acted on it, you are absolute responsibility, you had the courage to behave like a murderer in the eyes of the world and of your loved ones, in the eyes of morality, politics, and of the generality of the general or of your kind [*du générique*]. And you had even renounced hope.

Abraham is thus at the same time the most moral and the most immoral, the most responsible and the most irresponsible of men, absolutely irresponsible because he is absolutely responsible, absolutely irresponsible in the face of men and his family, and in the face of the ethical, because he responds absolutely to absolute duty, disinterestedly and without hoping for a reward, without knowing why yet keeping it secret; answering to God and before God. He recognizes neither debt nor duty to his fellows because he is in a relationship with God—a relationship without relation because God is absolutely transcendent, hidden, and secret, not giving any reason he can share in exchange for this doubly given death, not sharing anything in this dissymmetrical covenant. Abraham considers himself to be all square. He acts as if he were discharged of his duty toward his fellows, his son, and humankind; but he continues to love them. He must *love* them and also *owe* them everything in order to be able to sacrifice them. Without being so, then, he nevertheless feels absolved of his duty toward his family, toward the human species [*le genre humain*] and the generality of the ethical, absolved by the absolute of a unique duty that binds him to God the one. Absolute duty absolves him of every debt and releases him from every duty. Absolute ab-solution.

The ideas of secrecy and exclusivity [*non-partage*] are essential here, as is Abraham's silence. He doesn't speak, he doesn't tell his secret to his loved ones. He is, like the knight of faith, a witness and not a teacher (*Fear and Trembling*, 80), and it is true that this witness enters into an absolute relation with the absolute, but he doesn't witness to it in the sense that to witness means to show, teach, illustrate, manifest to others the truth that one can precisely attest to. Abraham is a witness of the absolute faith that cannot and must not witness before men. He must keep his secret. But his silence is not just any silence. Can one witness in silence? by silence?

The tragic hero, on the other hand, can speak, share, weep, complain. He doesn't know "the dreadful responsibility of loneliness" (114). Agamemnon can weep and wail with Clytemnestra and Iphigenia. "Tears and cries are relieving" (114); there is consolation in them. Abraham can neither speak nor commiserate, neither weep nor wail. He is kept in absolute secrecy. He feels torn, he would like to console the whole world, especially Sarah, Eliezer, and Isaac; he would like to embrace them before taking the final step. But he knows that they will then say to him, "But why are you doing that? Can't you get an exemption, find another solution, discuss, negotiate with God?" Or else they will accuse him of dissimulation and hypocrisy. So he can't say anything to them. Even if he speaks to them he can't say anything to them: " . . . he speaks no human language. And even if he understood all the languages of the world . . . he still could not speak—he speaks in a divine language, he speaks in tongues" (114). If he were to speak a common or translatable language, if he were to become intelligible by giving his reasons in a convincing manner, he would be giving in to the temptation of the ethical generality earlier referred to as that which makes one irresponsible. He wouldn't be Abraham any more, the unique Abraham in a singular relation with the unique God. Incapable of making a gift of death, incapable of sacrificing what he loved, hence incapable of loving and of hating, he wouldn't give anything anymore.

Abraham says nothing, but his last words, those that respond to Isaac's question, have been recorded: "God himself will provide the lamb for the holocaust, my son." If he had said "There is a lamb, I have one" or "I don't know, I have no idea where to find the lamb," he would have been lying, speaking in order to speak falsehood. By speaking without lying, he responds without responding. This is a strange responsibility that consists neither of responding nor of not responding. Is one responsible for what one says in an unintelligible language, in the language of the other? But besides that, mustn't responsibility always be expressed in a language that is foreign to what the community can already hear or understand only too well? "So he does not speak an untruth, but neither does he say anything, for he is speaking in a strange tongue" (119).

In Melville's "Bartleby the Scrivener," the narrator, a lawyer, cites Job ("with kings and counselors"). In spite of the obviously tempting comparison, the figure of Bartleby could be likened to Job—not to him who hoped to join the kings and counselors one day after his death, but to him who dreamed of not being born. Here, instead of the test to which God submits Job, one could think of that of Abraham. Just as Abraham doesn't speak a human language, just as he speaks in tongues or in a language that is foreign to every other human language, and in order to do that responds without responding, speaks without saying anything either true or false, says nothing determinate that would be equivalent to a statement, a promise, or a lie, in the same way Bartleby's "I would prefer not to" takes responsibility for a response without response. It evokes the future without either predicting or promising; it utters nothing fixed, determinable, positive or negative. The modality of this repeated utterance that says nothing, promises nothing, neither refuses nor accepts anything, the tense of this singularly insignificant statement, reminds one of a nonlanguage or a secret language. Is it not as if Bartleby were also speaking "in tongues"?

But for saying nothing general or determinable, Bartleby doesn't say absolutely nothing. *I would prefer not to* looks like an incomplete sentence. Its indeterminacy creates a tension: it opens onto a sort of reserve of incompleteness; it announces a temporary or provisional reserve, one involving a proviso. Can we not find there the secret of a hypothetical reference to some indecipherable providence or prudence? We don't know what he wants or means to say, or what he doesn't want to do or say, but we are clearly given to understand that *he would prefer not to*. The silhouette of a content haunts this response. If Abraham has already consented *to make a gift of death*, and to give to God the death that he is going to put his son to, if he knows that he will do it unless God stops him, can we not say that his disposition is such that he would, precisely, *prefer*

75

not to, without being able to say to the face of the world what is involved? Because he loves his son, he would prefer that God hadn't asked him anything. He would prefer that God didn't let him do it, that he would hold back his hand, that he would provide a lamb for the holocaust, that the instant of this mad decision—once the sacrifice had been accepted—would lean on the side of nonsacrifice. He will not decide *not to*, he has decided *to*, but he would prefer *not to*. He can say nothing more and will do nothing more if God, if the Other continues to lead him toward death, to the death that is offered as a gift. And Bartleby's "I would prefer not to" is also a sacrificial passion that will lead him to death, a death given by the law, by a society that doesn't even know why it is acting the way it does.

It is difficult not to be struck by the absence of woman in these two monstrous yet banal stories. It is a story of father and son, of masculine figures, of hierarchies among men: God the father, Abraham, Isaac. The woman, Sarah, is she to whom nothing is said, not to mention Hagar; and "Bartleby the Scrivener" doesn't make a single allusion to anything feminine whatsoever, and that is all the more the case for anything that could be construed as a figure of woman. Would the logic of sacrificial responsibility within the implacable universality of the law, of its law, be altered, inflected, attenuated, or displaced, if a woman were to intervene in some consequential manner? Does the system of this sacrificial responsibility and of the double "gift of death" imply at its very basis an exclusion or sacrifice of woman? A woman's sacrifice or a sacrifice of woman, according to one sense of the genitive or the other? Let us leave the question in suspense. Right here, between one genitive and another. In the case of the tragic hero or the tragic sacrifice, however, woman is decidedly present, her place is central, just as she is present in other tragic works referred to by Kierkegaard.

The responses without response made by Bartleby are at the same time disconcerting, sinister, and comical; superbly, subtly so. There is concentrated in them a sort of sublime irony. Speaking in order not to say anything or to say something other than what one thinks, speaking in such a way as to intrigue, disconcert, question, or have someone or something else speak (the law, the lawyer), means speaking ironically. Irony, in particular Socratic irony, consists in not saying anything, in not stating any knowledge, but it means doing that in order to interrogate, to have someone or something speak or think. *Eirōneia* dissimulates, it is the act of questioning by feigning ignorance, by pretending. *I would prefer not to* is not without irony; it cannot not lead one to suppose that there is some irony in the situation. It isn't unlike the incongruous yet familiar humor, the *unheimlich* or uncanniness of the story. On the other hand, the author of *The Concept of Irony* uncovers irony in the response without response that translates Abraham's responsibility. Precisely in order to distinguish ironic pretense from a lie, he writes,

> But a final word by Abraham has been preserved, and insofar as I can understand the paradox, I can also understand Abraham's total presence in that word. First and foremost, he does not say anything, and in that form he says what he has to say. His response to Isaac is in the form of irony, for it is always irony when I say something and still do not say anything. (118)

Perhaps irony would permit us to find something like a common thread running through the questions I have just posed, especially in the light of what Hegel said about woman: that she is "the eternal irony of the community."[5]

Abraham doesn't speak in figures, fables, parables, metaphors, ellipses, or enigmas. His irony is metarhetorical. If he knew what was going to happen, if for example God had charged him with the mission of leading Isaac onto the mountain so that he could strike him with lightning, then he would have been right to have recourse to enigmatic language. But the problem is precisely that he doesn't know. Not that he hesitates, however. His nonknowledge doesn't in any way suspend his own decision, which remains resolute. The knight of faith must not hesitate. He accepts his responsibility by heading off toward the absolute request of the other, be-

5. In this regard, I refer the reader to my *Glas*, trans. John P. Leavey, Jr., and Richard Rand (Lincoln: University of Nebraska Press, 1986), 190ff.

yond knowledge. He decides, but his absolute decision is neither guided nor controlled by knowledge. Such, in fact, is the paradoxical condition of every decision: it cannot be deduced from a form of knowledge of which it would simply be the effect, its conclusion or explicitation. It structurally breaches knowledge and is thus destined to nonmanifestation; a decision is, in the end, always secret. It remains secret in the very instant of its performance, and how can the concept of decision be dissociated from this figure of the instant? from the stigma of its punctuality?

Abraham's decision is absolutely responsible because it answers for itself before the absolute other. Paradoxically, it is also irresponsible because it is guided neither by reason nor by an ethics justifiable before men or before the law of some universal tribunal. Everything takes place as though one were unable to be responsible at the same time before the other and before others, before the others of the other. If God is the wholly other, the figure, or name of the wholly other, then every other (one) is every (bit) other. *Tout autre est tout autre.* This formula disturbs Kierkegaard's discourse on one level while at the same time reinforcing its most extreme ramifications. It implies that God, as wholly other, is to be found everywhere there is something of the wholly other. And since each of us, every one else, each other is infinitely other in its absolute singularity, inaccessible, solitary, transcendent, nonmanifest, originarily nonpresent to my *ego* (as Husserl would say of the *alter ego* that can never be originarily presented to my conscience and that I can apprehend only through what he calls *appresentation* and analogy), then what can be said about Abraham's relation to God can be said about my relation without relation to *every other (one) as every (bit) other* [*tout autre comme tout autre*], in particular my relation to my neighbor or my loved ones who are as inaccessible to me, as secret, and as transcendent as Jahweh. Every other (in the sense of each other) is wholly other (absolutely other). From this point of view what *Fear and Trembling* says about the sacrifice of Isaac is the truth. Translated into this extraordinary story, the truth is shown to possess the very structure of the everyday. Through its paradox it speaks of the responsibility required at every moment for every man and every woman. At the same time, there is no longer any ethical generality that does not fall prey to the paradox of Abraham.[6] At the instant of every decision and through the relation to *every other (one) as every (bit) other*, every one else asks us at every moment to behave like knights of faith. Perhaps that displaces a certain consequence of Kierkegaard's discourse: the absolute uniqueness of Jahweh doesn't tolerate analogy; we are not all Abrahams, Isaacs, or Sarahs either. We are not Jahweh. But what seems thus to universalize or disseminate the exception or the extraordinary by imposing a supplementary complication upon ethical generality, that very thing ensures that Kierkegaard's text gains added force. It speaks to us of the paradoxical truth of our responsibility and of our relation to the *gift of death* of each instant. Furthermore, it explains to us its own status, namely its ability to still be legible to all of us at the very moment when it is speaking of secrets in secret, of illegibility and absolute indecipherability. It stands for Jews, Christians, Muslims, but also for every one else, for every other in its relation to the wholly other. We no longer know who is called Abraham, and he can no longer even tell us.

Whereas the tragic hero is great, admired, and legendary from generation to generation, Abraham, in remaining faithful to his singular love for the wholly other, is never considered a hero. He doesn't make us shed tears and doesn't inspire admiration: rather

6. This is the logic of an objection made by Lévinas to Kierkegaard: "The ethical means the general for Kierkegaard. The singularity of the *I* would be lost, in his view, under a rule valid for all. Generality can neither contain nor express the *I*'s secret. Now, it is not at all certain that ethics is where he sees it. Ethics as consciousness of a responsibility toward others . . . far from losing you in generality, singularizes you, poses you as a unique individual, as *I*. . . . In his evocation of Abraham, he describes the encounter with God at the point where subjectivity rises to the level of the religious, that is to say, above ethics. But one could think the opposite: Abraham's attentiveness to the voice that led him back to the ethical order, in forbidding him to perform a human sacrifice, is the highest point in the drama. . . . It is here, in ethics, that there is an appeal to the uniqueness of the subject, and a bestowal of meaning to life, despite death." (Emmanuel Lévinas, *Proper Names*, trans. Michael B. Smith [Stanford: Stanford University Press, 1996], 76–77.) Lévinas's criticism doesn't prevent him from admiring in Kierkegaard "something absolutely new to European philosophy," "a new modality of the True," "the idea of persecuted truth" (77–79).

stupefied horror, a terror that is also secret. For it is a terror that brings us close to the absolute secret, a secret that we share without sharing it, a secret between an other, Abraham as the other, and another, God as the other, as wholly other. Abraham himself is in secret, cut off both from man and from God.

There we perhaps have what we share with him. But what does it mean to share a secret? Here it isn't a matter of knowing what the other knows, for Abraham doesn't know anything. It isn't a matter of sharing his faith, for the latter must remain an initiative of absolute singularity. And moreover, we don't think or speak of Abraham from the point of view of a faith that is sure of itself, any more than did Kierkegaard. Kierkegaard keeps coming back to this, recalling that he doesn't understand Abraham, that he wouldn't be capable of doing what he did. Such an attitude in fact seems the only possible one; and even if it is the most widely shared idea in the world, it seems to be necessitated by this monstrosity of such prodigious proportions. Our faith is not assured because a faith never can be, it must never be a certainty. We share with Abraham what cannot be shared, a secret we know nothing about, neither him nor us. To share a secret is not to know or to reveal the secret, it is to share we know not what: nothing that can be known, nothing that can be determined. What is a secret that is a secret about nothing and a sharing that doesn't share anything?

Such is the secret truth of faith as absolute responsibility and as absolute passion, the "highest passion" as Kierkegaard will say; it is a passion that, sworn to secrecy, cannot be transmitted from generation to generation. In this sense it has no history. This untransmissibility of the highest passion, the normal condition of a faith which is thus bound to secrecy, nevertheless dictates to us the following: we must always start over. A secret can be transmitted, but in transmitting a secret as a secret that remains secret, has one transmitted at all? Does it amount to history, to a story? Yes and no. The epilogue of *Fear and Trembling* repeats sentence after sentence that this highest passion that is faith must be started over by each generation. Each generation must begin again to involve itself in it without counting on the generation before. It thus describes the nonhistory of repeated absolute beginnings, and the very historicity that presupposes a tradition to be reinvented each step of the way, in this incessant repetition of the absolute beginning.

With *Fear and Trembling*, we hesitate between generations in the lineage of the so-called religions of the Book: we hesitate at the heart of the Old Testament and of the Jewish religion, but also the heart of a founding event or a key sacrifice for Islam. As for the sacrifice of the son by his father, the son sacrificed by men and finally saved by a God that seemed to have abandoned him or put him to the test, how can we not recognize there the foreshadowing or the analogy of another passion? As a Christian thinker, Kierkegaard ends by re-inscribing the secret of Abraham within a space that seems, in its literality at least, to be evangelical. That doesn't necessarily exclude a Judaic or Islamic reading, but it is a certain evangelical text that seems to orient Kierkegaard's interpretation. That text isn't cited; rather, like the Bartleby's "kings and counselors," it is simply suggested, but this time without the quotation marks, a clear reminder to those who know their texts and have been brought up on the reading of the Gospels:

> But there was no one who could understand Abraham. And yet what did he achieve? He remained true to his love. But anyone who loves God needs no tears, no admiration; he forgets the suffering in the love. Indeed, so completely has he forgotten it that there would not be the slightest trace of his suffering left if God himself did not remember it, *for he sees in secret* and recognizes distress and counts the tears and forgets nothing.
>
> Thus, either there is a paradox, that the single individual stands in an absolute relation to the absolute, or Abraham is lost. (120, my emphasis)

FOUR

Tout autre est tout autre

The danger is so great that I excuse the suppression of the object.
BAUDELAIRE, "The Pagan School"

. . . Christianity's *stroke of genius* . . .
NIETZSCHE, *The Genealogy of Morals*

"Every other (one) is every (bit) other"—the stakes seem to be altered by the trembling of this formula. It is no doubt too economical, too elliptical, and hence, like any formula, so isolated and capable of being transmitted out of its context, too much like the coded language of a password. One uses it to play with the rules, to cut someone or something short, to aggressively circumscribe a domain of discourse. It becomes the secret of all secrets. Is it not sufficient to transform what one complacently calls a context in order to demystify the shibboleth or decipher all the secrets of the world?

Is not this formula—*tout autre est tout autre*—in the first place a tautology? It doesn't signify anything that one doesn't already know, if by that one simply refers to the repetition of a subject in its complement, and if by so doing, one avoids bringing to bear upon it an interpretation that would distinguish between the two homonyms *tout* and *tout*, one an indefinite pronominal adjective (some, someone, some other one) and the other an adverb of quantity (totally, absolutely, radically, infinitely other). But after appealing to the supplement of a contextual sign in order to distinguish between the two grammatical functions and the two senses of what appears to be the same word (*tout*), one must also get around to distinguishing between the two *autres*. If the first *tout* is an indefinite pronominal adjective, then the first *autre* becomes a noun, and the second, in all probability, an adjective or attribute. One escapes the tautology but instead utters a radical heterology, the very proposition of the most irreducible heterology. Or else as a further alternative one might consider that in both cases (tautology and heterology, homonym or not) the two *autres* are finally repeated in the monotony of a tautology that wins out after all, the monotony of a principle of identity which, thanks to the copula and sense of being, would here take over alterity itself, nothing less than that, in order to say: the other is the other, that is always so, the alterity of the other is the alterity of the other. And the secret of the formula would close around a heterotautological speculation that always risks meaning nothing. But we know from experience that the speculative always requires a heterotautological position. That is its definition according to Hegel's speculative idealism, and it is the impetus for the dialectic within the horizon of absolute knowledge; which means, let us not forget, absolute philosophy as truth of a revealed religion that is precisely Christian. The heterotautological position introduces the law of speculation, and of speculation on every secret.

Let us not play at turning this little sentence around in order to make it dazzle from every angle. We would pay only slight and bemused attention to this particular formula and to the form of this key if, in the discreet displacement that affects the functions of the two words, there didn't appear, as if on the same musical scale, two alarmingly different renditions [*partitions*] that are in fact, through their disturbing likeness, incompatible.

One of them keeps in reserve the possibility of reserving the quality of the wholly other, in other words the *infinitely other*, for God alone, or in any case for a single other. The other attributes this infinite alterity of the wholly other to every other, in other words, recognizes it in each, each one, for example each man and woman, indeed each living thing, human or not. Even in its critique of Kierkegaard concerning ethics and generality Lévinas's thinking stays within the game—the play of difference and analogy—between the face of God and the face of my neighbor, between the infinitely other as God and the infinitely other as another human.[1] If every human is wholly other, if everyone else, or every other one, is every bit other, then one can no longer distinguish between a claimed generality of ethics that would need to be sacrificed in sacrifice, and the faith that turns toward God alone, as wholly other, turning away from human duties. But since Lévinas still wants to distinguish between the infinite alterity of God and the "same" infinite alterity of every human, or of the other in general, then he cannot simply say something different from Kierkegaard either. Neither one nor the other can assure himself of a concept of the ethical and of the religious that is of consequence; and consequently they are especially unable to determine the limit between those two orders. Kierkegaard would have to admit, as Lévinas recalls, that ethics is also the order of and respect for absolute singularity, and not only that of the generality or of the repetition of the same. He can therefore no longer distinguish so conveniently between the ethical and the religious. But for his part, in taking into account absolute singularity, that is to say the absolute alterity obtaining in relations with another human, Lévinas is no longer able to distinguish between the infinite alterity of God and that of every human: his ethics is already a religion. In both cases the border between the ethical and the religious becomes more than problematic, as do all discourses referring to it.

This is all the more so for political or legal matters. The general concept of responsibility, like that of decision, would thus be found to lack coherence or consequence, and even to lack identity with respect to itself, paralyzed by what can be called an aporia or an antinomy. That has never stopped it from "functioning," as one says, on the contrary. It operates so much better to the extent that it serves to obscure the abyss or fill in its absence of foundation, stabilizing a chaotic becoming in what are called conventions. Chaos refers precisely to the abyss or the open mouth, that which speaks as well as that which signifies hunger. What is thus found at

1. Cf. chapter 3, note 6; and "Violence and Metaphysics," in *Writing and Difference*, trans. Alan Bass (Chicago: University of Chicago Press, 1978), 96, 110ff.

work in everyday discourse, in the exercise of justice, and first and foremost in the axiomatics of private, public, or international law, in the conduct of internal politics, diplomacy, and war, is a lexicon concerning responsibility that can be said to hover vaguely about a concept that is nowhere to be found, even if we wouldn't go so far as to say that it doesn't correspond to any concept at all. It amounts to a disavowal whose resources, as one knows, are inexhaustible. One simply keeps on denying the aporia and antinomy, tirelessly, and one treats as nihilist, relativist, even poststructuralist, or worse still deconstructionist, all those who remain concerned in the face of such a display of good conscience.

The sacrifice of Isaac is an abomination in the eyes of all, and it should continue to be seen for what it is—atrocious, criminal, unforgivable; Kierkegaard insists on that. The ethical point of view must remain valid: Abraham is a murderer. However, is not the spectacle of this murder, which seems untenable in the dense and rhythmic briefness of its theatrical moment, at the same time the most common event in the world? Is it not inscribed in the structure of our existence to the extent of no longer even constituting an event? It will be said that it would be most improbable for the sacrifice of Isaac to be repeated in our day; and it certainly seems that way. We can hardly imagine a father taking his son to be sacrificed on the top of the hill at Montmartre. If God didn't send a lamb as a substitute or an angel to hold back his arm, there would still be an upright prosecutor, preferably with expertise in Middle Eastern violence, to accuse him of infanticide or first-degree murder; and if a psychiatrist who was both a little bit psychoanalyst and a little bit journalist were to declare that the father was "responsible," carrying on as if psychoanalysis had done nothing to upset the order of discourse on intention, conscience, good will, etc., the criminal father would have no chance of getting away with it. He might claim that the wholly other had ordered him to do it, and perhaps in secret (how would he know that?), in order to test his faith, but it would make no difference. Everything is organized to insure that this man would be condemned by any civilized society. On the other hand, the smooth functioning of such a society, the monotonous complacency [*ronronnement*] of its discourses on morality, politics, and the law, and the very exercise of its rights (whether public, private, national, or international), are in no way perturbed by the fact that, because of the structure of the laws of the market that society has instituted and controls, because of the mechanisms of external debt and other comparable inequities, that same "society" *puts to death* or (but failing to help someone in distress accounts for only a minor difference) *allows to die* of hunger and disease tens of millions of children (those relatives or fellow humans that ethics or the discourse of the rights of man refer to) without any moral or legal tribunal ever being considered competent to judge such a sacrifice, the sacrifice of the other to avoid being sacrificed oneself. Not only does such a society participate in this incalculable sacrifice, it actually organizes it. The smooth functioning of its economic, political, and legal order, the smooth functioning of its moral discourse and good conscience, presuppose the permanent operation of this sacrifice. And such a sacrifice is not even invisible, for from time to time the television displays—while keeping them at a distance—a series of intolerable images of it, and a few voices are raised to bring it all to our attention. But those images and voices are completely powerless to induce the slightest effective change in the situation, to assign the least responsibility, to furnish anything other than alibis. That this order is founded upon a bottomless chaos (the abyss or open mouth) is something that will necessarily be brought home one day to those who just as necessarily forget the same. We are not even talking about wars, the least recent or most recent ones, in which cases one can wait an eternity for morality or international law (whether violated with impunity or invoked hypocritically) to determine with any degree of rigor who is responsible or guilty for the hundreds of thousands of victims who are sacrificed for what or whom one knows not, countless victims, each of whose singularity becomes each time infinitely singular—every other (one) being every (bit) other—whether they be victims of the Iraqi state or victims of the international coalition that accused that state of not respecting the law. For in the discourses that dominated during such wars, it was rigorously impossible, on one side and the other, to discern the religious from the moral, the juridical from the political. The warring factions were all irreconcilable fellow worshipers of the religions of the Book. Does that not make things converge once again in the fight to the death previously referred to, which continues to rage on Mount Moriah over possession of the secret of the sacrifice by an Abraham who never said anything? Do they not fight in order to appropriate the secret as the sign of their covenant with God, and impose its order on the other, who becomes for his part nothing more than a murderer?

The trembling of the formula "every other (one) is every (bit) other" can also be reproduced. It can do so to the extent of replacing one of the "every other's" by God: "Every other (one) is God," or "God is every (bit) other." Such a substitution in no way alters the "extent" of the original formulation, whatever grammatical function be assigned to the various words. In one case God is defined as infinitely other, as the wholly other. In the other case it is declared that every other one, each of the others, is God inasmuch as he or she is, *like* God, wholly other.

Are we just playing here? If this were a game, then it would need to be kept safe, unscathed, like the game that must be kept alive [*qu'il faut sauver*] between humans and God. For the game between these two unique "every other's," like the same "every other," opens the space or introduces the hope of salvation, the economy of "saving oneself" that we shall shortly discuss. Linking alterity to singularity or to what one could call the universal exception, or the rule of the exception (*tout autre est tout autre* signifies that every other is singular, that "every" is a singularity, which also means that every is each one, a proposition that seals the contract between universality and the exception of singularity, that of "no matter who"), this play of words seems to contain the very possibility of a secret that hides and reveals itself at the same time within a single sentence and, more than that, within a single language. Or at least within a finite group of languages, within the finitude of language as that which opens onto the infinite. The essential and abyssal equivocality, that is to say the play of the several senses of *tout autre est tout autre* or *Dieu est tout autre*, is not, in its literality (that of French or Italian, for example), universally translatable, presuming one continues to trust a traditional concept of translation. The sense of the play can no doubt be translated by a paraphrase into other languages, but

not the formalizing economy of the slippage between two homonyms in the language that can here be called singularly my own
(with its use of *tout* as indefinite pronominal adjective and as adverb, and *autre* as indefinite pronominal adjective and as noun).
We have here a kind of *shibboleth*, a secret formula such as can be
uttered only in a certain way in a certain language. As a chance or
aleatory effect, the untranslatability of this formal economy functions like a secret within one's so-called natural or mother tongue.
One can regret such a limiting function or on the contrary take
pride in it; one can derive some national prestige from it, but either
way there is nothing to be done or said about such a secret of the
mother tongue. It is there before us in its possibility, the *Geheimnis* of language that ties it to the home, to the motherland, to the
birthplace, to economy, to the law of the *oikos*, in short to the family and to the family of words derived from *heim*, home, *heimlich*,
unheimlich, *Geheimnis*, etc.

What might this secret of the mother tongue have to do with
the secret that the father sees in, as the Gospel according to Saint
Matthew puts it, which Kierkegaard refers to at the end of *Fear and
Trembling*? There is a secret of the mother tongue, the secret that
the father's lucidity sees in, and the secret of the sacrifice of Isaac.
It is indeed an economy, literally a matter of the law (*nomos*) of the
home (*oikos*), of the family and of its hearth and focus [*foyer*]; and
of the space separating or associating the fire of the family hearth
and the fire of the sacrificial holocaust. A double focus or hearth,
a double fire and double light; two ways of loving, burning, and
seeing.

To see in secret—what can that mean?

Before recognizing there a quote from the Gospel according to
Saint Matthew (*videre in abscondito / en tō kryptō blepein*), let us note
that the penetration of the secret is entrusted to the gaze, to sight,
to observation, rather than to hearing, smelling, or touching. One
might imagine a secret that could only be penetrated or traversed,
undone or opened as a secret, by hearing, or one that would only
allow itself to be touched or felt, precisely because in that way it
would escape the gaze or be invisible, or indeed because what was
visible in it would keep secret the secret that wasn't visible. One can

always expose to sight something that still remains secret because its secret is accessible only to senses other than sight. For example, writing that I can't decipher (a letter in Chinese or Hebrew, or simply some undecipherable handwriting) remains perfectly visible in spite of being in the main sealed. It isn't hidden but it is encoded or encrypted. That which is hidden, as that which remains inaccessible to the eye or the hand, is not necessarily encrypted in the derivative senses of that word—ciphered, coded, to be interpreted—in contrast to being hidden in the shadows (which is what it also meant in Greek).

What should we make of the slight difference that appears in the Gospel between Greek on the one hand, and the Latin of the Vulgate on the other? In *in abscondito, absconditus* refers rather to the hidden, the secret, the mysterious as that which retreats into the invisible, that which is lost from sight. The majority of examples or figures on the basis of which *absconditus* has come to mean secrecy in general, and so has become synonymous with *secretum* (separate, retired, withdrawn from view), privilege the optical dimension. The absolute sense of what withdraws from view is not necessarily, of course, that of a visible that conceals itself, for example my hand under the table—my hand as such is visible but I can render it invisible. The absolute sense of invisibility resides rather in the idea of that which has no structure of visibility, for example the voice, what is said or meant, and sound. Music is not invisible is the same way as a veiled sculpture. The voice is not invisible in the same way as skin under clothing. The nudity of a timbre or a whisper doesn't have the same quality as the nudity of a man's or woman's breast; it signifies neither the same modesty nor the same invisibility. In contrast to *absconditus* (not to mention *mystique*), the Greek lexicon referring to the cryptic (*kryptō, kryptos, kryptikōs, kryphios, kryphaiōs,* etc.), while of course also signifying the concealed, dissimulated, secret, clandestine, etc., seems rather to make reference in a less strict, less manifest way, to sight. It extends beyond the visible. And in this semantic history, the cryptic has come to enlarge the field of secrecy beyond the nonvisible toward whatever resists deciphering, the secret as illegible or undecipherable rather than invisible.

Nevertheless, if the two senses communicate so easily, if they can be translated one within the other or one into the other, then perhaps, among other reasons, it is because of the fact that the invisible can be understood, let us say, in *two ways*.

1. There is a visible in-visible, an invisible of the order of the visible that I can keep secret by keeping it out of sight. This invisible can be artificially kept from sight while remaining within what one calls exteriority. (If I hide a nuclear arsenal in underground silos or hide explosives in a cache, there is a still a surface involved; and if I hide a part of my body under clothing or a veil, it is a matter of concealing one surface beneath another; whatever one conceals in this way becomes invisible but remains within the order of visibility; it remains constitutively visible. To take another set of examples, in the same way but according to a different structure, what one calls the interior of the body—my heart, my kidneys, my blood, my brain—are, one says, naturally invisible, but they are still of the order of visibility: an operation or accident can expose them to the surface, their interiority is provisional, their invisibility can be promised or proposed to sight.) All that is of the order of the visible in-visible.

2. But there is also absolute invisibility, the absolutely nonvisible that refers to whatever falls outside the register of sight, namely the sonorous, the musical, the vocal, or phonic (and hence the phonological or discursive in the strict sense), but also the tactile or the odoriferous. And desire, like curiosity, like the experience of modesty [*pudeur*] and the unclothing of secrecy, the revealing of the *pudenda* or the fact of "seeing in secret (*videre in abscondito*)," all those movements that take secrecy beyond the secret necessarily come into play. But they can come into play only within the scale of the invisible: the invisible as concealed visible, the encrypted invisible or the nonvisible as that which is other than visible. This is an immense problem that appears both classic and enigmatic, yet each time as if afresh, and we can merely draw attention to it here. When Kierkegaard–de Silentio makes a barely veiled reference to the Gospel of Matthew, the allusion to "your father who sees in secret (*qui videt in abscondito / ho blepōn en tō kryptō*)" echoes on more than one stave within that scale.

In the first place, the allusion describes a relation to the wholly other, hence an absolute dissymmetry. It is all that suffices to provoke the *mysterium tremendum*, inscribing itself within the order of the gaze. God sees me, he looks into me in secret, but I don't see him, I don't see him see me, even though he sees me facing me and not like an analyst on whom I will have turned my back. Since I don't see him see me, I can, or must, only hear him. But most often I have to be led to hear him, by insinuation [*on doit me le donner à entendre*], I hear tell or hear myself say what he says through the voice of another, another other, a messenger, an angel, a prophet, a messiah, or a postman, a bearer of tidings, an evangelist, an intermediary who speaks between God and myself. There is no face-to-face exchange of looks between God and myself, between the other and myself. God looks at me and I don't see him, and it is on the basis of this gaze that singles me out [*ce regard qui me regarde*] that my responsibility comes into being. Thus, in fact, is instituted or revealed the "it concerns me" or "it's my lookout" [*ça me regarde*], which leads me to say "it is my business, my affair, my responsibility." But not in the sense of a (Kantian) autonomy by means of which I see myself acting in total liberty and according to a law that I make for myself; rather in the heteronomy of an "it's my lookout" even when I can't see anything, don't know anything, and can take no initiative, there where I cannot preempt by my own initiative whatever is commanding me to make decisions, decisions that will nevertheless be mine and which I alone will have to answer for.

It is dissymmetrical: this gaze that sees me without my seeing it see me. It knows my very secret even when I myself don't see it and even though the Socratic "Know yourself" seems to install the philosophical within the lure of reflexivity, in the disavowal of a secret that is always *for me*, that is to say, *for the other*: *for me* who never sees anything in it, and hence *for the other* alone, to whom, through the dissymmetry, a secret is revealed. For the other my secret will no longer be a secret. The two uses of "for" don't have the same sense: at least in this case the secret for me is what I can't see; the secret for the other is what is revealed only to the other, which she alone can see. By disavowing this secret, philosophy would have come to inhabit the misunderstanding of what there is to know, namely that there is secrecy and that it is incommensurable with knowing, with knowledge, and with objectivity, as in the incommensurable "subjective interiority" that Kierkegaard extracts from every knowledge relation of the subject/object type.

How can another see into me, into my most secret self, without my being able to see in there myself and without my being able to see him in me? And if my secret self, that which can be revealed only to the other, to the wholly other, to God if you wish, is a secret without reflexivity, one that I will never know or experience or reappropriate as my own, then what sense is there in saying that it is "my" secret, a secret "of mine," or in saying more generally that a secret *belongs*, that it is proper to or belongs to some "one," or to some *other* who remains some*one*? It is perhaps there that we find the secret of secrecy, namely that there is no knowledge of it and it is there for no one. A secret doesn't belong, it can never be said to be at home or in its place [*chez soi*]. Such is the *Unheimlichkeit* of the *Geheimnis* and we need to systematically question the reach of the former concept such as functions, in a regulated manner, in two systems of thought that extend equally, although in different ways, beyond an axiomatic of the self or the *chez soi* as *ego cogito*, as consciousness or representative intentionality, for example, and in an exemplary fashion, in Freud and Heidegger. The question of the self: "who am I?" no longer in the sense of "who am I" but "who is this 'I'" that can say "who"? What is the "I" and what becomes of responsibility once the identity of the "I" trembles *in secret*?

This dissymmetry of the gaze leads us back to what Patočka suggests concerning sacrifice and back to the tradition of the *mysterium tremendum*. In spite of the opposition that seems to obtain between *Fear and Trembling* and the Kantian logic of autonomy, of a pure ethics or practical reason that is exceeded by absolute duty as it extends into the realm of sacrifice, Kierkegaard still follows the latter tradition. Access to pure duty is, in Kant's terms, also "sacrifice," the sacrifice of the passions, of the affections, of so-called "pathological" interests; everything that links my sensibility to the empirical world, to calculation, and to the conditionality of hypothetical imperatives. The unconditionality of respect for the law also dictates a sacrifice (*Aufopferung*) which is always a sacrifice of self (even for Abraham when he gets ready to kill his son; he inflicts the most severe suffering upon himself, he gives to himself the death that he is granting his son and also giving, in another way, to God; he puts his son to death or grants him death and offers the death so given to God). According to Kant the unconditionality of moral law dictates the violence that is exercised in self-restraint (*Selbstzwang*) and against one's own desires, interests, affections, or drives. But one is driven to sacrifice by a sort of practical drive, by a form of motivation that is also instinctive [*pulsionnel*], but in the sense of a pure and practical instinct, respect for moral law being its sensitive point. The *Critique of Practical Reason* (chapter 3, "Of the Motives (*Triebfedern*) of Pure Practical Reason") closely links the *Aufopferung*, sacrifice of self, to obligation, debt, and duty, which are never separable from guilt (*Schuldigkeit*), from that with which one is never quits, which one can never acquit oneself of or settle.

Patočka describes the coming of Christian subjectivity and the repression of Platonism through recourse to a figure that faces us, one might say, with a sacrifice that is inscribed within the dissymmetry of looks that cannot be exchanged. He does so literally, and, let us remember, on at least two occasions: "*Tremendum*, for responsibility is now vested not in a humanly comprehensible essence of goodness and unity but, rather, in an inscrutable relation to the absolute highest being in whose hands we are not externally, but internally" (106). This is the moment where the light or sun of the Good, as invisible source of intelligible visibility, but which is not itself an eye, goes beyond philosophy to become, in the Christian faith, a gaze. A personal gaze, that is, a face, a figure, and not a sun. The Good becomes personal Goodness, and a gaze that sees me without my seeing it. A little later there is this "suppression of the object," as Baudelaire might have put it: "In the final analysis, the soul is not a relation to an *object*, however noble (like the Platonic Good) but rather to a Person who sees into the soul without being itself accessible to view. What a Person is, that really is not adequately thematized in the Christian perspective" (107).

This look that cannot be exchanged is what situates originary culpability and original sin; it is the essence of responsibility. But at the same time responsibility sets in train the search for salvation through sacrifice. The word "sacrifice" is used a little further on, in the context of Judeo-Christianity (Patočka's single reference in this essay to the Old Testament), and of the being-toward-death, of what we are here calling the apprehension of the gift of death, or death as an offering:

> an openness to the abyss in the divine and the human, to the wholly unique and so definitively self-determining bond of divinity and humanity, the unique drama to which the fundamental content of the soul relates throughout. The transcendent God of antiquity combined with the Old Testament Lord of History becomes the chief personage in the inner drama which God makes into the drama of salvation and grace. The overcoming of everydayness assumes the form of the care for the salvation of the soul which won itself in a moral transformation, in the turn in the face of death and death eternal; which lives in anxiety and hope inextricably intertwined, which trembles in the knowledge of its sin and with its whole being offers itself in the sacrifice of penance. (117)

As we were saying earlier, a *general economy of sacrifice* could be deployed according to several forms of "logic" or "calculation." At their limits, calculation, logic, and even economy in the strict sense point precisely to what is at stake, suspended, or *epochalized* in such an *economy of sacrifice*.[2] Through their differences these economies perhaps perform decipherings of what is one and the *same* economy. But "amounting to the same thing," like economy, could also be an inexhaustible operation.

At the moment when Kierkegaard concludes by re-Christianizing or pre-Christianizing the sacrifice of Isaac with such determination, as if *preparing* for Christianity, he implicitly refers to the Gospel of Matthew: "For he (God the Father) sees in secret and

2. Concerning this economy of sacrifice, I refer the reader once again to *Glas*, notably 32–33, 41ff. (on Hegel, Abraham, the "sacrifice" of Isaac and the "economic simulacrum"), 68ff., 96, 108, 119, 123, 139–41, 155ff., 207–8, 235, 240–43, 253ff., 259ff.; and to "Economimesis," trans. Richard Klein, *Diacritics* 11.2 (1981).

recognizes distress and counts the tears and forgets nothing" (*Fear and Trembling*, 120). God sees in secret, he knows. But it is as if he didn't know what Abraham was going to do, or decide, or decide to do. He gives him back his son after assuring himself that Abraham has trembled, renounced all hope, and irrevocably decided to sacrifice his beloved son to him. Abraham had consented to suffer death or worse, and that without calculating, without investing, beyond any perspective of reappropriation; hence, it seems, beyond recompense or retribution, beyond economy, without any hope of remuneration [*salaire*]. The sacrifice of economy, that without which there is no responsibility that is free and relative to decision (a decision always takes place beyond calculation), is indeed in this case the sacrifice of the *oikonomia*, namely of the law of the home (*oikos*), of the hearth, of what is one's own or proper, of the private, of the love and affection of one's kin. This is the moment when Abraham gives the sign of absolute sacrifice, namely by putting to death or giving death to his own, putting to death his absolute love for what is dearest, his only son; this is the instant in which the sacrifice is all but consummated—for no more than an instant, a *no-time-lapse*, separates the raised arm of the murderer from murder itself—the impossible-to-grasp instant of absolute imminence in which Abraham can no longer go back on his decision, nor even suspend it. *In this instant*, therefore, in the imminence that no longer even separates the decision from the act, God gives him back his son and decides by sovereign decision, by an absolute gift, to reinscribe sacrifice within an economy by means of what thenceforth resembles a reward.

On the basis of the Gospel of Matthew we can wonder what "to give back" or "to pay back" [*rendre*] means ("thy Father which seeth in secret shall reward thee [*reddet tibi/apodōsei soi*]").[3] God decides to *give back*, to give back life, to give back the beloved son, once he is assured that a gift outside of any economy, the gift of death—and of the death of that which is priceless—has been accomplished without any hope of exchange, reward, circulation, or

---

3. The French translates the Latin and Greek more literally than the English as (*il*) *te le rendra* ("he will give it back to you" or "he will pay you back").—Trans.

communication. To speak of the secret between God and Abraham is to also say that, in order that there be this gift as sacrifice, all communication between them has to be suspended, whether communication as exchange of words, signs, sense, or promise, or communication as exchange of goods, things, riches, or property. Abraham renounces all sense and all property—that is where the responsibility of absolute duty begins. Abraham is in a relation of nonexchange with God, he is in secret since he doesn't speak to God and expects neither response nor reward from him. The response and hence responsibility always risk what they cannot avoid appealing to *in return*, namely recompense and retribution. They risk the exchange that they should at the same time expect and fail to count on, hope for yet exclude.

It is finally in renouncing life, the life of his son that one has every reason to think is more precious than his own, that Abraham gains or wins. He risks winning; more precisely, having renounced winning, expecting neither response nor recompense, expecting nothing that can be *given back* to him, nothing that will *come back* to him (when we once defined dissemination as "that which doesn't come back to the father," we might as well have been describing the instant of Abrahamic renunciation), he sees God give back to him, in this instant of absolute renunciation, the very thing that he had already, in the same instant, decided to sacrifice. It is given back to him because he has renounced calculation. Demystifiers of this superior or sovereign calculation that consists in no more calculating might say that he played his cards well. Through the law of the father economy reappropriates the *an*economy of the gift as a gift of life or, what comes down to the same thing, a gift of death.

Let us come back to Matthew (chap. 6). On three occasions a truth is repeated, like some obsessive reminder to be learned by heart. It is the sentence "and thy Father which seeth in secret shall reward thee (*reddet tibi / apodōsei soi*)." It is a truth "to be learned by heart" in the first place because one has the impression of having to learn it without understanding it, like a repeated and repeatable formula (like our *tout autre est tout autre* just now, a sort of obscure proverb that one can transmit and transport without understanding it, like a sealed message that can be passed from hand to hand or whispered from mouth to ear). It is a matter of learning "by heart" beyond sense. God is in fact asking that one give without knowing, without calculating, reckoning, or hoping, for one must give without counting, and that is what takes it outside of sense. But we say "to be learned by heart" for another reason. This passage is also a meditation or sermon on the heart, on what the heart is and more precisely what it *should be* should it return to its correct place. The essence of the heart, that is to say where the heart is what it must properly be, where it properly takes place, in its correct *site [emplacement]*, that is the very thing that gives us food for thought concerning economy. For the place of the heart is, or rather is called or destined to be, the place of true riches, a place of treasure, the placement of the greatest *thesaurization* or laying up of treasures. The correct site of the heart is the place of the best placement.

This passage from the Gospels concentrates, as we know, on the question of justice, and especially what we might call economic justice: alms-giving, wages, debt, laying up of treasures. Now the line demarcating celestial from terrestrial economy is what allows one to situate the correct place of the heart. One must not lay up treasures for oneself on earth but in heaven. After saying for the third time, here on the mountain, "and thy Father which seeth in secret shall reward thee" (in other words "you can count on the economy of heaven if you sacrifice the earthly economy"), Jesus teaches as follows:

> Lay not up for yourselves treasures upon earth (*Nolite thesaurizare vobis thesauros in terra*), where moth and rust doth corrupt, and where thieves break through and steal.
>
> But lay up for yourselves treasures in heaven (*Thesaurizate autem vobis thesauros in caelo*), where neither moth nor rust doth corrupt, and where thieves do not break through and steal.
>
> For where treasure is, there will your heart be also (*Ubi enim est thesaurus tuus, ibi est cor tuum / hopou gar estin thesauros sou, ekei estai kai he kardia sou*). (Matthew 6:19–21)

Where is the heart? What is the heart? The heart will thus be, in the future, wherever you save real treasure, that which is not visible on earth, that whose capital accumulates beyond the economy of the terrestrial visible or sensible, that is to say beyond the corrupted or corruptible economy vulnerable to moth, rust, and thieves. What is implied here is more than the pricelessness of celestial capital. It is invisible. It doesn't devalue, it can never be stolen from you. The celestial coffers are more secure, unbreakable, out of reach of any forced entry or ill-conceived market gamble. This capital, unable to be devalued, can only yield an infinite profit; it is an infinitely secure placement, better than the best, a chattel without price.

As an economic discourse on the site or placement of the heart this cardiotopology is also an ophthalmology. The celestial treasure is invisible to corrupted and corruptible eyes of flesh. There is the good and simple eye (*oculus simplex* / *ophthalmos haplous*), and the bad, corrupt, or depraved (*nequam* / *poneros*) eye:

> The light of the body is the eye (*Lucerna corporis tui est oculus tuus* / *Ho lukhnos tou somatos estin ho ophthalmos*): if therefore thine eye be single (*simplex* / *haplous*—the Grosjean and Léturmy French translation gives "healthy" [*sain*]), thy whole body shall be full of light.
>
> But if thine eye be evil, thy whole body shall be full of darkness. If therefore the light that is in thee be darkness, how great is that darkness. (Matthew 6:22–23)

The organ of sight begins by being a source of light. The eye is a lamp. It doesn't receive light, it gives it rather. It is not that which receives or regards the Good from the outside, or outwardly, as solar source of visibility; it gives light from the inside. It is therefore the Good become goodness, the becoming-good of the Good, since it lights from the interior, from the inside of the body, namely the soul. However, although it is internal in its source, this light doesn't belong to this world or this earth. It can seem obscure, somber, nocturnal, secret, invisible to eyes of flesh, to corrupted eyes, and that is where "seeing in secret" becomes necessary. In this way God the Father reestablishes an economy that was interrupted by the dividing of heaven from earth.

This passage from the Gospel of Matthew deals with justice, with what it is to be just or to do justice (*justitiam facere/dikaiosynēn poiein*). Jesus had praised the poor in spirit (*pauperes spiritu/ptōkhoi tō pneumati*: beggars in spirit). The sermon is organized around the question of poverty, begging, alms, and charity, of what it must mean to give *for Christ*, of what giving means *to Christ*, and what it means to give *for Christ*, to him, in his name, for him, in a new fraternity with him and on his terms, as well as what it means to be just in so giving, for, in, and according to Christ. The kingdom of heaven is promised to the poor in spirit who are blessed, elated [*dans l'allégresse*] (*beati/makarioi*), along with them that mourn, the meek, them which do hunger and thirst after righteousness, the merciful, the pure in heart, the peacemakers, those persecuted for righteousness' sake, those reviled for God's sake. All of those are promised remuneration, a reward, a token (*merces/misthos*), a good salary, a great reward (*merces copiosa/misthos polus*), *in heaven*. In this way real heavenly treasure is constituted, on the basis of the salary or price paid for sacrifice or renunciation on earth, and more precisely on the basis of the price paid to those who have been able to raise themselves above the earthly or literal justice of the Scribes and Pharisees, the men of letters, of the body and of the earth. If your justice does not exceed that of the Scribes and Pharisees or the men of letters, as opposed to those of the spirit, you will not enter the kingdom of heaven. One can translate that as follows: you won't receive your wages (*mercedem*).

A *logic* is therefore put in place. One can note certain of its characteristics.

A. *On the one hand*, we have here a *photology* in terms of which the source of light comes from the heart, from inside; from the spirit and not from the world. After saying "Ye are the salt of the earth," Christ says in the same breath, "Ye are the light of the world (*lux mundi/phōs tou kosmou*)," and "A city that is set on an hill cannot be hid (*abscondi/krybenai*)" (Matthew 5:14). A mutation takes place in the history of secrecy. If the light was in the world, if it had its source on the outside and not within us, within the spirit, one would be able to conceal objects, cities, or nuclear arms. The object wouldn't be suppressed, simply hidden behind a screen.

Only an apparatus of this world would be required to create secret places. A *thing* would be protected by another, sheltered behind or beneath *something*; apparatuses, caches, or crypts would be constructed and the secret would be kept invisible. But once the light is in us, within the interiority of the spirit, then secrecy is no longer possible. This sort of omnipresence is more radical, effective, and undeniable than that of a spy satellite that turns, as one says, "in space." Nothing sensible or terrestrial would be able to stand in its way. There would be no obstacle to interrupt the gaze.

The interiorization of the photological source marks the end of secrecy, but it is also the origin of the paradox, that of the secret as irreducibly interior. No more secrecy means more secrecy [*plus de secret, plus de secret*]: that is another secret of secrecy, another formula or shibboleth that depends entirely on whether or not you pronounce the final *s* of *plus*, a distinction that cannot be made *literally*.[4] *There where, wherever*, and more precisely—since place no longer takes place—*as soon as* there is no longer any secret hidden from God or from the spiritual light that passes through every space, then a recess [*retrait*] of spiritual subjectivity and of absolute interiority is constituted allowing secrecy to be formed within it. Subtracted from space, this incommensurable inside of the soul or the conscience, this inside without any outside carries with it both the end and the origin of the secret. *Plus de secret.* For if there were no absolutely heterogeneous interiority outside of objectivity, if there were no nonobjectifiable inside, there would be no secrecy either. Whence the strange economy of the secret as economy *of* sacrifice that is installed here. And again, there is an instability in the grammatical play of the genitive in this expression or *formula* "economy of sacrifice": one economizes thanks to sacrifice and one economizes sacrifice; it is a sacrifice that economizes or an economy that sacrifices.

B. *On the other hand*, if this spiritualization of the "interior" light institutes a new economy (an economy of sacrifice: you will receive

---

4. The final *s* of *plus* is pronounced in the expression *plus de secret* to mean "more secret(s)/secrecy" and not pronounced when it means "no more secret(s)/secrecy."—Trans.

good wages if you rise above earthly gain, you will get a better salary if you give up your earthly salary, one salary is waged against
another), then it is by breaking with, dissociating from, or rendering dissymmetrical whatever is paired with the sensible body, just as
it means breaking with exchange as a simple form of reciprocity. In
the same way as it will be said, to prevent reinscribing alms-giving
within a certain economy of exchange, "But when thou doest alms,
let not thy left hand know what thy right hand doeth" (6:3), so also:
"if thy right eye offend [*scandalise*] thee, pluck it out, and cast it
from thee" (5:29). And the same goes for the hand:

> Ye have heard that it was said by them of old time, Thou
> shalt not commit adultery:
>
> But I say unto you, That whosoever looketh on a woman
> to lust after her hath committed adultery with her already
> in his heart.
>
> And if thy right eye offend (*scandalizat / skandalizei*: the
> *skandalon* is what makes one fall, stumble, sin) thee, pluck
> it out, and cast it far from thee: for it is profitable for thee
> that one of thy members should perish, and not that thy
> whole body should be cast into hell.
>
> And if thy right hand offend thee, cut it off, and cast it
> from thee: for it is profitable for thee that one of thy mem-
> bers should perish, and not that thy whole body should be
> cast into hell. (Matthew 5:27–30)

Such an economic calculation integrates absolute loss. It breaks
with exchange, symmetry, or reciprocity. Granted, absolute subjectivity has come to restart a calculus or infinite raising of the stakes
within the terms of an economy of sacrifice, but this is by sacrificing sacrifice understood as finite commerce. There is *merces*, wages,
merchandizing if not mercantilism; there is payment, but not commerce if commerce presupposes the reciprocal *and finite* exchange
of wages, merchandise, or reward. The dissymmetry signifies that
different economy of sacrifice which, a little later, will allow Christ
to say, still talking about the eye, about the right and the left, about
breaking up a pair or pairing up:

Ye have heard that it hath been said, An eye for an eye (*oculum pro oculo / ophthalmon anti ophthalmou*), and a tooth for a tooth:

But I say unto you, That ye resist not evil (*non resistere malo / mē antistēnai tō ponerō*): but whosoever shall smite thee on thy right cheek, turn to him the other also. (5:38–39)

Does this commandment reconstitute the parity of the pair rather than breaking it up, as we just suggested? No, it doesn't, it interrupts the parity and symmetry, for instead of *paying back* the slap on the cheek (right cheek for right cheek, eye for eye), one is to *offer* the other cheek. It is a matter of suspending the strict economy of exchange, of payback, of giving and getting back, of tit for tat [*un prêté pour un rendu*], of that hateful roundabout of reprisal, vengeance, blow for blow, settling scores. So what are we to make of this economical symmetry of exchange, of give and take and of paying back, once it is said, a little further on, that God the Father who sees in secret, will reward you or pay you back for it (*reddet tibi*)? The logic that commands us to suspend the reciprocity of vengeance and not to resist evil is naturally the logic, the *logos* itself, which is life and truth, namely Christ, who, as Patočka's "goodness that forgets itself," teaches love for one's enemies. For it is precisely in this passage that he says, "Love your enemies . . . pray for them which . . . persecute you," etc. (*Diligite inimicos vestros / agapate tous ekhthrous humōn*) (5:44). It is more necessary than ever to quote the Latin or Greek, if only in consideration of the remark made by Carl Schmitt when, in chapter 3 of *The Concept of the Political*, he emphasizes the fact that *inimicus* is not *hostis* in Latin and *ekhthros* is not *polemios* in Greek. This allows him to conclude that Christ's teaching concerns the love that we must show to our private enemies, to those we would be tempted to hate through personal or subjective passion, and does not suppose that love is owed to a public enemy. (Schmitt recognizes in passing that the distinctions between *inimicus* and *hostis* and between *ekhthros* and *polemios* have no strict equivalent in other languages, at least not in German.) Christ's teaching would thus be moral or psychological, even metaphysical, but not political, which is important for Schmitt, for whom a particular war waged against a determinate enemy (*hostis*), a war or hostility that doesn't presuppose any hate, would be the condition for the emergence of the political. As he reminds us, no Christian politics ever advised the West to love the Muslims who invaded Christian Europe.

This again raises, among other things, the question of a Christian politics, one that conforms to the gospels. For Schmitt, but in a very different sense from Patočka, a Christian or European-Christian politics seems possible. The modern sense of the political itself would be tied to such a possibility inasmuch as political concepts are secularized theologico-political concepts. But for that to be so we must presume Schmitt's reading of "love your enemies" to be immune from any discussion, and more importantly from any contestation of what might be called an ethnophilological type, since the war waged against the Muslims, to cite but a single case, was a political fact in his sense, confirming the existence of a Christian politics, of a coherent design in genuine agreement with the Gospel of Matthew, capable of bringing all Christians and the whole Church together in a spirit of consensus. But one can doubt that, just as we can find ourselves perplexed by the reading of "love your enemies and pray for those who persecute you." For the text says,

> Ye have heard that it hath been said, Thou shalt love thy neighbor, and hate thine enemy.
>
> But I say unto you, Love your enemies, bless them that curse you, do good to them that hate you, and pray for them which despitefully use you, and persecute you. (5:43–44)

When Jesus says "Ye have heard that it hath been said, Thou shalt love thy neighbor, and hate thine enemy," he refers in particular to Leviticus 19:15–18, at least in the first part of the sentence ("Thou shalt love thy neighbor"), if not the second ("hate thine enemy"). Indeed, there it is said, "Thou shalt love thy neighbor as thyself." But in the first place, vengeance is already condemned in Leviticus and the text doesn't say "thou shalt hate thine enemy." In the second place, since it defines the neighbor in the sense of fellow creature [*congénère*], as a member of the same ethnic group (*'amith*), we are already in the sphere of the political in Schmitt's sense. It would seem difficult to keep the potential opposition between one's neighbor and one's enemy within the sphere of the private. The passage from Leviticus sets forth a certain concept of justice. God is speaking to Moses, to whom he has just given a series of prescriptions concerning sacrifice and payment, and, it needs to be underlined, he forbids revenge:

> I am the Lord.
> Ye shall do no unrighteousness in judgment: thou shalt not respect the person of the poor, nor honor the person of the mighty: but in righteousness shalt thou judge thy neighbor.
> Thou shalt not go up and down as a talebearer among the people: neither shalt thou stand against the blood of thy neighbor: I am the Lord.
> Thou shalt not hate thy brother in thine heart: thou shalt in any wise rebuke thy neighbor, and not suffer sin upon him.
> *Thou shalt not avenge*, nor bear any grudge against the children of thy people, but thou shalt love thy neighbor as thyself: I am the Lord. (Leviticus 19:14–18)

If one's neighbor is here one's *congener*, someone from *my* community, from the same people or the same nation (*'amith*), then the person who can be opposed to him or her (which is not what Leviticus, but indeed what the Gospel does) is the non-neighbor not as private enemy but as foreigner, as member of another nation, community, or people. That runs counter to Schmitt's interpretation: the frontier between *inimicus* and *hostis* would be more permeable than he wants to believe. At stake here is the conceptual and practical possibility of founding politics or of forming a rigorous concept of political specificity by means of some dissociation: not only that between public and private but also between public existence and the passion or shared community affect that links each of its members to the others, as with members of the same family, the same ethnic, national, or linguistic community, etc. Is national or nationalist affect, or community affect, political in itself, or not? Is it public or private according to Schmitt? It would be difficult to answer the question, and to do so would require a new elaboration of the problematic.

Immediately following the "Love your enemies," the Gospel of Matthew again refers to wages or salary (*mercedem/misthon*). Once again, and once already, for the question of remuneration will permeate the discourse on God the Father who sees in secret and who will reward you (by implication with a salary). We need to distinguish between two types of salary: one of retribution, equivalent exchange, within a circular economy; the other of absolute surplus value, heterogeneous to outlay or investment. Two seemingly heterogeneous economies therefore, but in any case two types of wages, two types of *merces* or *misthos*. And the opposition between the mediocre wages of retribution by exchange, and the noble salary that is obtained through disinterested sacrifice or though the gift, also points to a difference between two peoples, ours, to whom Christ is speaking, and the others, who are referred to as *ethnici* or *ethnikoi*, the ethnicities therefore, in short the peoples, those who are only peoples, collectivities [*grégarités*] (*goyim* in André Chouraqui's French translation, "pagans" in Grosjean and Léturmy's Bibliothèque de la Pléiade version). Let us not forget the use of the word "pagan," for it will shortly further advance our reading. Here is the end of chapter 5 of the Gospel according to Saint Matthew:

> But I say unto you, Love your enemies, bless them that curse you, do good to them that hate you, and pray for them which despitefully use you, and persecute you;
>
> That ye may be the children of your Father which is in heaven: for he maketh his sun to rise on the evil and on the good, and sendeth rain on the just and on the unjust.
>
> For if ye love them which love you, what reward have ye (*Si enim diligitis eos qui vos diligunt, quam mercedem habebitis / ean gar agapēsete tous agapōntas humas, tina misthon ekhete*)? Do not even the publicans the same? (44–46)

Something passes from one father to another, but authentic filiation is reinstated ("that ye may be children of your Father"). It occurs on condition that there is a gift, a love *without reserve*. If you love only those who love you and to the extent that they love you, if you hold so strictly to this symmetry, mutuality, and reciprocity, then you give nothing, no love, and the reserve of your wages will be like a tax that is imposed or a debt that is repaid, like the acquittal of a debt. In order to deserve or expect an infinitely higher salary, one that goes beyond the perception of what is due, one has to give without taking account and love those who don't love you. It is here that reference is made to "ethnic groups" or "pagans":

> And if you salute your brethren only, what do ye more *than others*? Do not even the Gentiles (*ethnici/ethnikoi*) so? (5:47)[5]

This infinite and dissymmetrical economy of sacrifice is opposed both to that of the Scribes and Pharisees, to the old law in general, and to that of heathen ethnic groups or gentiles (*goyim*); it is on the one hand Christian in contrast to Judaic, on the other hand Judeo-Christian. It always presumes a calculation that claims to go beyond calculation, beyond the totality of the calculable as a finite totality of the same. Granted, there is an economy, but it is an economy that integrates the renunciation of a calculable remuneration, renunciation of merchandise or bargaining, of economy in the sense of a retribution that can be measured or made symmetrical. In the space opened by this economy of what is without measure, a new teaching of the gift or of alms-giving still relies on *giving back* or *paying back* [*rendre*], on a yield [*rendement*], even a profitability [*rentabilité*], of course, but creatures cannot calculate the latter and must leave it to the appreciation of *the father as he who sees in secret*. Starting from chapter 4 of the same Gospel, the theme of justice is at least appealed to—even if neither marked nor remarked upon—being named precisely as that which must be practiced without being marked or remarked upon. One must be just without being noticed for it. To want to be noticed means

5. In French, *les païens*, "pagans," "heathens." "Gentiles" is from the Revised Standard Version; King James repeats "publicans" (*telōnai*) as in verse 46. Both exist in different versions of the Greek.—Trans.

wanting recognition and payment in the form of a calculable salary, in the form of thanks [*remerciement*] or recompense. On the contrary, one must give, alms for example, without knowing, or at least by giving with one hand without the other hand knowing, that is to say without having it known, without having it known by other men, in secret, without counting on recognition, reward, or remuneration. Without even having it known to oneself. The dissociation between right and left again breaks up the pair, the parity or pairing, the symmetry between, or homogeneity of two economies. It interrupts all the way to self-consciousness, and in fact inaugurates sacrifice. But an infinite calculation takes over from the finite calculating that has been renounced. God the Father, who sees in secret, will pay back your salary, and on an infinitely greater scale.

Have things become clearer? Perhaps, except for the divine clarity on whose secrecy light does not have to be shed:

> Take heed that ye do not your alms before men, to be seen of them: otherwise ye have no reward of your Father which is in heaven.
>
> Therefore when thou doest thine alms, do not sound a trumpet before thee, as the hypocrites do in the synagogues and in the streets, that they may have glory of men. Verily I say unto you, They have their reward.
>
> But when thou doest alms, let not thy left hand know what thy right hand doeth:
>
> That thine alms may be in secret; and thy Father which seeth in secret himself shall reward thee openly. (Matthew 6:1–4)

This promise is repeated several times in a similar form, whether it concern alms, prayer, or fasting (6:6, 17–18). The clarity of divine lucidity penetrates everywhere yet keeps within itself the most secret of secrets. In order to eschew idolatrous or iconic simplisms, that is to say visible images and ready-made representations, it might be necessary to understand this sentence ("and thy Father which seeth in secret . . . shall reward thee") other than as a proposition concerning what God might be, this subject, entity, or X that on the one hand would already exist, and who, on the other hand, what is more, would be endowed with attributes such as paternity and the power to penetrate secrets, to see the invisible, to see in me better than I, to be more powerful and more intimate with me than myself. We should stop thinking about God as someone, over there, way up there, transcendent, and, what is more—into the bargain, precisely—capable, more than any satellite orbiting in space, of seeing into the most secret of the most interior places. It is perhaps necessary, if we are to follow the traditional Judeo-Christian-Islamic injunction, but also at the risk of turning it against that tradition, to think of God and of the name of God without such a representation or such idolatrous stereotyping. Then we might say: God is the name of the possibility I have of keeping a secret that is visible from the interior but not from the exterior. As soon as such a structure of conscience exists, of being-with-oneself, of speaking, that is to say of producing invisible sense, as soon as I have within me, *thanks to the invisible word as such*, a witness that others cannot see, and who is therefore *at the same time other than me and more intimate with me than myself*, as soon as I can have a secret relationship with myself and not tell everything, as soon as there is secrecy and secret witnessing within me, and for me, then there is what I call God, (there is) what I call God in me, (it happens that [*il y a que*]) I call myself God—a phrase that is difficult to distinguish from "God calls me," for it is on such a condition that I can call myself or be called in secret. God is in me, he is the absolute "me" or "self," he is that structure of invisible interiority that is called, in Kierkegaard's sense, subjectivity. And he is made manifest, he manifests his non-manifestation when, in the structures of the living or the existent, in the course of phylo- and ontogenetic history, there appears the possibility of secrecy, however differentiated, complex, plural, and overdetermined it be; that is to say when there appears the desire and power to render absolutely invisible and to constitute within oneself a witness of that invisibility. That is the history of God and of the name of God as the history of secrecy, at the same time secret and without any secrets. Such a history is also an economy.

Another economy? Perhaps the same one in simulacrum, an economy that is ambiguous enough *to seem* to integrate noneconomy. In its essential instability the same economy seems sometimes faithful to, and sometimes accusing or ironic with respect to Christian sacrifice. It begins by denouncing an offering that still appears too calculating; one that would renounce earthly wages (*merces*) and a finite, accountable, exterior, visible market, one that would exceed an economy of retribution and exchange (the *re-merciement*), only to capitalize on it by means of a profit or surplus value that was infinite, heavenly, incalculable, interior, and secret. A sort of secret calculation would continue to wager on the gaze of a God who sees the invisible, and who sees in my heart what I decline to have seen by my fellow humans.

Of spirit—spirit itself. "The Spirit of Christianity," to quote the title of an essay by a youthful Hegel, who recognized in the *manifestation* of this revealed religion, in its coming about, the announcement of its own truth, namely absolute knowledge; a potential omnipotence, the dynasty of a Christianity that no longer knows any limit and gnaws at its frontiers, attaining its invincibility at the cost of knowing how to conquer *itself*: the power to get carried away with itself [*s'emporter soi-même*, also "win out over itself"] in the secret market of secrecy. "*Christianity's* stroke of genius," as Nietzsche will say next, perhaps still being naïve enough to believe he knows, at the moment he parodies the literary text by Chateaubriand, what is meant by *to believe*, *to lead to believe*, or *to give credit to*, in this onward march or merchandising of the infinite. Christianity's relation to itself, its self-affirmation or self-presentation, its being-*self*, is constituted in the hyperbole of this market, in the visibility of the invisible heart. There could not then be any "external" critique of Christianity that was not the extension of an internal *possibility* and that did not reveal the still intact *powers* of an unforeseeable future, of an event or *worldwide* advent of Christianity. There would therefore be here no pertinent external or internal critique that did not miss its target, quite simply for having first incorporated it. Every demystification of Christianity submits again and again [*se plie et replie*] to justifying a proto-Christianity to come.

A (hi)story of men. This potential [*réserve*] is kept in the fold of a sacrifice without sacrifice, at the instant that saves, or if one prefers, resuscitates the son: Isaac, Ishmael, and Jesus are all brothers in the end. Each time a son, the son, the only one. At the expense of Sarah, Hagar, and Ishmael. Should it be said that these three, and everything they were to represent in the future, were the first to be sacrificed?[6]

Each time *the* son is lost and saved *by* the father, by *th*e father alone. A story of men.

In the fold of this Abrahamic or Ibrahimic moment, folded back by the Gospel between the two other "religions of the book," in the recess [*repli*] of this fathomless secret, there would be announced the *possibility* of the fiction nicknamed literature: its *possibility* rather than the event of its *institution*, its structural accommodation but by no means yet what readies and in*states* it [*la* met en État], or confers upon it the status it derives from that name, which is a modern sequence, barely a few centuries old. We would be tempted to maintain, contrary to what is often assumed to be the case, that the identifiable origin of this young institution—like that of the modern figure of the democratic state—is more Abrahamic than Greek, something we shall return to in the essay that follows. For the moment, let us simply signal this one among its traits: from out of the strange and impossible filiation that we detect in it, in memory of so many fathers and sons, and in memory of so many more men who have been ready—without ever managing it, perhaps without ever believing in it—to give themselves a gift of death to the death [*à se donner la mort à mort*], this institution at least retains the feature that we would characterize, after Baudelaire, as that of appearing always as a "homicidal and suicidal literature." A (hi)story of men and not of women; a story of "fellow men" [*semblables*]. A history of fraternity and a history of Christianity: "Hypocritical reader, my fellow, my brother."

The literary hyperbole of this critique of Christianity, which is at the same time evangelical and heretical, is illustrated in a short

6. "The abandoned Hagar, and her child, never stop haunting what the word *islam* sought to define," notes Fethi Benslama, thus recalling and analyzing "Hagar's eviction within the foundation of Islam." I can but refer the reader to his admirable article, "La répudiation originaire," in *Idiomes, Nationalités, Déconstructions: Rencontre de Rabat avec Jacques Derrida* (Casablanca: Éditions Toukbal, 1998).

pamphlet by Baudelaire, "The Pagan School" (1852). For the reasons that we have just recalled, and because it is hyperbolic, this "critique" is unable to be simply internal or external. In a few intemperate pages, his verve and anger project a poetics, a morality, a religion, and a philosophy. First among the accused are certain unnamed writers (probably Banville and others, like Leconte de Lisle and Gautier, who celebrated Greek culture and its models).[7] Declaring himself against the cult of form and plasticity of those he calls the neopagans, who are at the same time idolatrous, materialist, and formalist, Baudelaire warns against the prostitution of those who kneel before the aestheticism of representation, against the materialism of the image, of appearances and of idolatry, against the literal exteriority of appearing (elsewhere he won't fail to support the opposite, according to a controlled set of paradoxes). Speaking of alms a little in the manner of Matthew's Gospel, he ends up by recounting a story of counterfeit money that is simpler, more impoverished, and less perverse in its structure than "Counterfeit Money," but still close enough to call for a serial type of analysis. And he "excuses the suppression of the object":

> Impossible to take a step, to speak a word without stumbling into something pagan. . . . And you, miserable neopagans, what are you doing if not the same thing? . . . Apparently you have lost your soul somewhere. . . . To dismiss passion and reason is to kill literature. To repudiate the efforts of a preceding society, Christian and philosophic, is to commit suicide. . . . To surround oneself exclusively with the charms of material art is to run the risk of damnation. For a long time, a very long time, you will be able to see, love and feel only the beautiful, and nothing but the beautiful. I am using the word in a restricted sense. The world will appear to you only in its material form. . . . May religion and philosophy come one day as if compelled by the cry of a despairing soul. Such will always be the fate of

7. Théodore de Banville, Charles-Marie Leconte de Lisle, and Théophile Gautier.

madmen who see in nature only forms and rhythms. Even philosophy will at first appear to them as only an interesting game. . . . His soul [that of the child so corrupted], constantly excited and unappeased, goes about the world, the busy, toiling world . . . like a prostitute crying: Plastic! Plastic! The plastic—that frightful word gives me goose flesh—the plastic has poisoned him, and yet he can live only by this poison. . . . I understand the rage of iconoclasts and Moslems against images. I admit all the remorse of Saint Augustine for the too great pleasure of the eyes. The danger is so great that I excuse the suppression of the object. The folly of art is equal to the abuse of the mind. The creation of one of these two supremacies results in foolishness, hardness of heart and in enormous pride and egoism. I recall having heard an artist, who was a practical joker and who had received a false coin, say on one occasion: I shall keep it for some poor person. The wretch took an infernal pleasure in robbing the poor and in enjoying at the same time the benefit of a reputation for charity. I heard someone else say: Why don't the poor wear gloves to beg? They would make a fortune. And another: Don't give anything to that one; his rags don't fit well; they aren't very becoming to him. . . . The time is not distant when it will be understood that every literature that refuses to walk hand in hand with science and philosophy is a homicidal and suicidal literature.[8]

This discourse seems to be of a piece and it is certainly less *rusé* than "Counterfeit Money." But it still lends itself to two readings. The evangelical spiritualist outbidding is constantly at risk of having its bluff called. "The Pagan School" can always unmask a sort of

8. Charles Baudelaire, "The Pagan School," in *Baudelaire as Literary Critic*, ed. and trans. Lois Boe Hyslop and Francis E. Hyslop, Jr. (University Park: Pennsylvania State University Press, 1964), 74–77. The allusion to the counterfeiter in "The Pagan School" was not taken into account in my reading of "Counterfeit Money" (cf. *Given Time. 1. Counterfeit Money*, trans. Peggy Kamuf [Chicago: University of Chicago Press, 1992]).

sublime and secret calculation in the salary promised in heaven by the Father who sees in secret and will pay it back, that of him who seeks to "win paradise economically" as the narrator of "Counterfeit Money" puts it. The moment the gift, however generous it be, is touched by the slightest hint of calculation, the moment it takes account of knowledge [*connaissance*] or recognition [*reconnaissance*], it allows itself to be caught in transacting: it exchanges, in short it gives counterfeit money, since it gives in exchange for payment. Even if it gives "true" money, the alteration of the gift into a form of calculation immediately destroys, as if from the inside, the value of the very thing that is given. The money may keep its value but it is no longer given as such. Once it is tied to remuneration (*merces*) it is counterfeit, because it is mercenary and mercantile; even if it is real. Whence the double "suppression of the object" that can be inferred by slightly displacing Baudelaire's formulation: as soon as it calculates (starting from the simple intention of giving *as such*, starting from sense, knowledge, and whatever takes recognition into account), the gift suppresses the object (of the gift). It denies it as such. In order to avoid this negation or destruction at all costs, one must proceed to *another* suppression of the object: that of keeping in the gift only the giving, the act of giving, and intention to give, not the given, which in the end doesn't count. One must give without knowing, without knowledge or recognition, without *thanks* [*remerciement*]: without anything, or at least without any object.

The critique or polemic of "The Pagan School" would have the virtue of *demystification*. The word is no longer fashionable but it does seem to impose itself in this case, does it not? It is a matter of unfolding the mystagogical hypocrisy of a secret, putting on trial a fabricated mystery, a contract with a secret clause, namely that, seeing in secret, God will pay back infinitely more; a mystery that we accept all the more easily since God remains the witness of every secret. He shares and *he knows*. We have to *believe* that he knows. This knowledge *at the same time* founds *and* destroys, *both* the Christian concepts of responsibility and justice, *and* their "object." The genealogy of responsibility that Nietzsche refers to in *The Genealogy of Morals* as "the long history of the origins of responsibility (*Verantwortlichkeit*)," also describes the filiations of moral and religious conscience: a theater of cruelty and sacrifice, even of the holocaust (these are Nietzsche's words), of fault as debt or obligation (*Schuld*, that "main moral concept," that *Hauptbegriff* of morality), placements of economy, of "the contractual relationships" between creditors (*Gläubiger*) and debtors (*Schuldner*). These relations appear as soon as there exist subjects under law in general (*Rechtssubjekte*), and they lead back in turn "to the basic forms of buying, selling, bartering, trade and traffic."[9]

Sacrifice, vengeance, cruelty, all that is inscribed in the genesis of responsibility and moral conscience. "The categorical imperative" of "old Kant" reeks of cruelty (45). But Nietzsche's diagnosis of cruelty is at the same time aimed at economy, speculation, and commercial trafficking (buying and selling) in the institution of morality and justice. It is also aimed at the "objectivity" of the object: "'every thing has its price: *everything* can be compensated for.'" This was "the oldest, most naïve canon of morals relating to *justice*, the beginning of all 'good naturedness,' 'equity,' all 'good will,' all 'objectivity' on earth" (50).

For Nietzsche goes so far as to take into account, as it were, the moment when this justice integrates what is nonsolvent, the unacquittable, the absolute. He thus takes into account that which exceeds economy as exchange, and the com*merce* of *re-merciement*. But instead of crediting that to pure goodness, to faith, or the infinite gift, he reveals in it, at the same time as the suppression of the object, a self-destruction of justice by means of grace. That is the properly Christian moment as self-destruction of justice:

> Justice, which began by saying, "Everything can be paid off, everything must be paid off," ends by turning a blind eye (*durch die Finger zu sehn*) and letting off those unable to pay,—it ends, like every good thing on earth, by *sublimating itself* [what is translated in the French as "destroying itself" is literally *sich selbst aufhebend*—and Nietzsche

9. Friedrich Nietzsche, *On the Genealogy of Morality*, trans. Carol Diethe (Cambridge: Cambridge University Press, 1994), 39, 43–44.

adds the emphasis: by "raising itself or by substituting for itself," Christian justice denies itself and so conserves itself in what seems to exceed it; it remains what it ceases to be, a cruel economy, a commerce, a contract involving debt and credit, sacrifice and vengeance]. The self-sublimation of justice (*Diese Selbstaufhebung der Gerechtigkeit*): we know what a nice name it gives itself—*Merci!* (*Gnade* ["grace"]); it remains, of course, the prerogative (*Vorrecht*) of the most powerful man, better still, his way of being beyond the law (*sein Jenseits des Rechts*). (51–52)

In its *Selbstaufhebung* justice remains a privilege, *Gerechtigkeit* remains a *Vorrecht* as that which is *Jenseits des Rechts*. That obliges us to think about what the *Selbst* represents in this *Selbstaufhebung* in terms of the constitution of the self in general, through this secret nucleus of responsibility.

In questioning a certain concept of repression (*Zurückschiebung*, "relegation," [67]) that moralizes the mechanism of debt[10] via moral duty and bad conscience, via conscience as guilt, one might proceed to track the hyperbolization of such a repression (perhaps bringing it to bear, in passing, upon what Patočka says about Christian repression). This sacrificial *hubris* is what Nietzsche calls "*Christianity's* stroke of genius." It is what takes this economy to its excess in the sacrifice of Christ for love of the debtor; it involves the same economy of sacrifice, the same sacrifice of sacrifice:

... that paradoxical and horrifying expedient through which a martyred humanity has sought temporary relief, *Christianity's* stroke of genius (*jenem Geniestreich des* Christentums): none other than God sacrificing himself for man's guilt, none other than God paying himself back, God as the only one able to redeem man from what, to man himself, has become irredeemable (*unablösbar*)—the creditor (*der Gläubiger*)

---

10. I have approached these passages from *The Genealogy of Morals* from a differ- . ent perspective in *The Post Card: From Socrates to Freud and Beyond*, trans. Alan Bass (Chicago: University of Chicago Press, 1987), notably 263–65.

sacrificing himself for his debtor (*seinen Schuldner*), out of love (would you credit it? [*sollte man's glauben?*]—), out of *love* for the debtor! . . . (68)

If there is such a thing as this "stroke of genius," it comes about only at the instant of the infinite sharing of the secret. If, like a thaumaturgical secret, like the technique of a power or the ruse of a know-how, one were able to attribute it to someone or something called "Christianity," one would have to envelop another secret within it: the reversal and infinitization that confers on God, on the other or on the name of God, the responsibility for that which remains more secret than ever, the irreducible experience of belief, between credit and faith, the *believing* [*croire*] suspended between the credit [*créance*] of the creditor (*Gläubiger*) and the credence ([*croyance*] *Glauben*) of the believer [*croyant*]. How can one *believe* this history of *credence* or *credit*? That is what Nietzsche asks, *in fine*, what he asks himself or has asked by another, by the specter of his discourse. Is this a false or counterfeit question, a rhetorical question as one says in English? For what makes a rhetorical question possible can sometimes disturb the structure of it.

As often happens, the call of or for the question, and the request that echoes through it, takes us further than the response. The question, the request, and the appeal *must* indeed have begun, since the eve of their awakening, by receiving accreditation from the other: by being believed. Nietzsche must indeed believe he knows what believing means, unless he means it to make-believe [*à moins qu'il n'entende le faire accroire*].

LITERATURE
IN SECRET

An Impossible Filiation

"God," if you'll pardon the expression . . .

JACQUES DERRIDA

TRANSLATED BY
DAVID WILLS

Pardon de ne pas vouloir dire.

Imagine that we were to leave this utterance to its fate.

Consent for a time at least to my abandoning it like that, alone, really exposed, aimless, wandering, erratic even: "Pardon for not meaning (to say)..."[1] Is this, such an utterance, a sentence? A phrase from a prayer? A request about which it is still too early, or already too late, to know whether it has simply been interrupted, whether it requires or excludes suspension points at the end? "Pardon for not meaning (to say) [...]"

Unless it were the case that I found it one day, such an improbable phrase, unless it were found, itself, alone, visible, and abandoned, at the mercy of every passerby, written on a board, readable

---

1. Consideration of Derrida's attention to the gift (*don*) and forgiveness (*le pardon*) recommends translating *pardon de ne pas vouloir dire* using "forgive" rather than "pardon." However, English would then require a personal pronoun (e.g., "forgive me for not saying"), which would anchor the phrase more than Derrida seems to want here. The reader should therefore hear "pardon" in the sense of "forgive."

Vouloir dire literally means "to want to say," but is also the everyday expression for "to mean." In order to suggest the semantic silence or secret of *dire* in the French phrase I have parenthesized "to say" in most cases where the expression is used.—Trans.

on a wall, inscribed in a stone, on the surface of a sheet of paper or saved, in reserve, on a computer disk.

Here then is the secret of a phrase: "Pardon for not meaning (to say)," it says [*dit-elle*, also "says she"].

"Pardon for not meaning (to say) . . ." has now become a quotation.

So the interpreter studies it.

An archeologist might well wonder if the phrase is complete: "Pardon for not meaning (to say) . . . ," but what in fact? And to whom? Who to whom?

There there is secrecy [*il y a là du secret*], and we sense that literature is taking over these words, without, for all that, appropriating them in order to fashion them to its own purpose.

The average hermeneut can't know whether this request ever signified something in a real context. Was it addressed one day by someone to someone, by a real signatory to a determinate addressee?

ONE

The Test of Secrecy: For the One as for the Other

Among all those, infinite in number throughout history, who have kept an absolute secret, a terrible secret, an infinite secret, I think of Abraham, starting point for all the Abrahamic religions, but also the origin of this fund without which what we call literature would probably never have managed to emerge as such and under that name. Does the secret of some elective affinity therefore ally the secret of the elective Covenant [*Alliance*] between God and Abraham with the secret of what we call literature, the secret *of* literature and secrecy *in* literature?

Abraham might have said, as might God also, "Pardon for not meaning (to say) . . ." I think of Abraham who kept the secret—speaking of it neither to Sarah nor even to Isaac—concerning the order given him, in tête-à-tête, by God. The sense of that order remained secret, even to him. All that we know is that it was a trial or test [*épreuve*, also "proof"]. What test? I would like to propose a reading of it, one that I will distinguish, in this case, from an interpretation. At the same time active and passive, this reading would be presumed by every interpretation, by the exegeses, commentaries, glosses, decipherings that have been accumulating in infinite numbers for thousands of years. As a result it would not be simply one interpretation among others. In both the fictive and nonfictive form that I plan to give to it, it would have the characteristics of a very strange sort of evidence or certainty. It would also have the clarity and distinction of being a secret experience concerning a secret. What secret? Well, the following one: unilaterally assigned by God, the test imposed on Mount Moriah would consist precisely in proving [*éprouver*] whether Abraham was capable of keeping a secret: in short, "of not meaning to say . . ." All the way to hyperbole, to the point where not meaning to say becomes so radical that it is almost confused with "not being able to mean (to say) [*ne pas pouvoir vouloir dire*]."

What would all that mean?

It is therefore indeed a question of a *test to prove* something, indubitably, and the word is agreed upon by all the translators:

> And it came to pass after these things, that God did tempt Abraham, and said unto him, Abraham: and he said, Behold *here* I *am*.[1]

(The request for secrecy begins in this instant: I pronounce your name, you sense yourself being called by me, you say "here I am" and by your response you commit yourself not to speak of us, of this exchange of words, where we give our word, to no one else, you commit to respond to me and to me alone, solely, to respond before me alone, and only me, in tête-à-tête, without a third party. You have already sworn, you are already committed to keeping the secret of our covenant, this call and this co-responsibility, between the two of us. The first breaking of an oath [*parjure*, "perjury," "forswearing"] would consist in betraying this secret.

But let us wait a little to see how this test of secrecy involves the sacrifice of what is dearest, the greatest love in the world, what is unique in love itself, one unique against another, one unique for another. For the secret of secrecy about which we shall speak does not consist in hiding *something*, in not revealing the truth, but in respecting the absolute singularity, the infinite separation of what

---

1. Genesis 22:1. Derrida is quoting from the French Pléiade edition, trans. E. Dhormes (Paris: Gallimard, 1972): "Il advint que L'Élohim éprouva Abraham . . ."; cf. Revised Standard Version: "After these things God tested Abraham . . ." —Trans.

binds me or exposes me to the unique, to one as to the other, to *the One as to the Other*):

> And he said, Take now thy son, thine only *son* Isaac, whom thou lovest, and get thee in to the land of Moriah; and offer him there for a burnt-offering upon one of the mountains that I will tell thee of.
>
> And Abraham rose up early in the morning and saddled his ass, and took two of his young men with him, and Isaac his son, and clave the wood for the burnt-offering, and rose up, and went into the place of which God had told him. (Genesis 22:2–3, my italics)[2]

Kierkegaard never stopped talking about Abraham's silence. His insistence in *Fear and Trembling* is a response to a strategy that deserves a long and detailed analysis all by itself; concerning notably the powerful conceptual and lexical inventions of the "poetic" and the "philosophical," of the "aesthetic," the "ethical," the "teleological," and the "religious." In particular, various *movements*, as I shall call them, in the musical sense, act in concert around this silence. Four lyrical movements of fictional narration, all of them addressed to Regine, in fact open the book. Such fables belong to what one would no doubt have the right to call literature. They recount or invent the biblical story in their own way. Let us underline the words that give rhythm to the resounding echo of these silences:

> They rode *in silence* for three days. On the morning of the fourth day Abraham *said not a word.* . . . But Abraham said

---

2. " 'Prends donc ton fils, ton unique, celui que tu aimes, Isaac, va-t'en au pays de Moriah et là offre-le en holocauste sur l'une des montagnes que je te dirai.' Abraham se leva de bon matin, sangla son âne, prit ses deux serviteurs avec lui, ainsi que son fils Isaac, fendit les bois de l'holocauste, se leva et s'en alla vers l'endroit que lui avait dit L'Élohim" (Dhormes). Another translation: "Et c'est après ces paroles: 'L'Elohîm éprouve Abrahâm. Il lui dit: Abrahâm! Il dit: Me voici. Il dit: Prends donc ton fils, ton unique, celui que tu aimes, Is'hac, va pour toi en terre de Moryah, là, monte-le en montée sur l'un des monts que je te dirai.' Abrahâm se lève tôt le matin et bride son âne. Il prend ses deux adolescents avec lui et Is'hac son fils. Il fend des bois de montée. Il se lève et va vers le lieu que lui dit L'Elohîm" (trans. Chouraqui [Paris: Desclée de Brouwer, 2001]).

to himself, "I will not hide from Isaac where this walk is taking him."

But he doesn't say anything to him, so that at the end of this *first movement*, one hears an Abraham who understands [*s'entend*] he is speaking only to himself or to God, within himself to God:

> But Abraham *said softly to himself*, "Lord God in heaven, I thank you; it is better that he believes me a monster than that he should lose faith in you."

Second movement:

> They rode along the road *in silence*. . . . *Silently* he arranged the firewood and bound Isaac; *silently* he drew the knife.

In the *fourth movement* the secret of silence is indeed shared by Isaac, but neither one nor the other ruptures the secret of what has happened; moreover, they have well and truly decided not to speak of it at all:

> Not a word is ever said of this in the world, and Isaac never talked to anyone about what he had seen, and Abraham did not suspect that anyone had seen it. (*Fear and Trembling*, 10–14)[3]

---

3. Kierkegaard speaks elsewhere of a "pledge [*voeu*] of silence" (21). And everything he calls the teleological suspension of the ethical will be determined by Abraham's silence, by his refusal of mediation, of the generality, of the law of the public (*juris publici*), of the political, of the state, of the divine. The divine is only the "phantom" of God (68), as the generality of the ethical is but the bloodless specter of faith. Abraham, on the other hand, is not, must not, cannot be "as phantom, a showpiece used for diversion" (53). Kierkegaard often repeats that Abraham *cannot* speak, insisting on this impossibility or in-capability [*im-pouvoir*]—insisting on "he cannot" before any "he will not"—for he is as if passive in his decision not to speak (113–15, and passim), in a silence that is no longer an aesthetic silence. The whole operative difference here is that between Abraham's paradoxical secret and the secret of what must be hidden in the aesthetic order but, on the contrary, revealed in the ethical order. Aesthetics demands the secret of what remains hidden and rewards it; ethics, for its part, requires instead its manifestation. Aesthetics cultivates the secret, ethics punishes it. Yet the paradox of faith is neither aesthetic (the desire to conceal) nor ethical (the interdiction against concealing) (cf. 82ff.). This paradox of faith will

The same secret, the same silence, therefore separates Abraham and Isaac. For what Abraham has not seen, or so the fable makes clear, is the fact that Isaac saw him, saw him draw his knife, saw his face wracked with despair. Abraham therefore doesn't know that he has been seen. He sees without seeing himself seen. In this regard he is in nonknowledge. He doesn't know that his son will have been his witness, even if a witness henceforth held to the same secret, the secret that binds him to God.

Is it therefore by chance that in one of these movements, within one of the four silent orchestrations of the secret, Kierkegaard imagines a great tragedy of forgiveness? How can one harmonize these themes of silence, secrecy, and forgiveness? In the *third movement*, after an enigmatic paragraph where the profiles of Hagar and Ishmael are seen passing furtively through Abraham's pensive reverie, the latter implores God. He throws himself on the ground and asks for God's forgiveness: not for having disobeyed him, but on the contrary for having obeyed him. And for having obeyed him at the moment when he was given an impossible order, a doubly impossible order: impossible both because the worst was being asked of him and because, in a movement that we will ourselves have reason to come back to, God will go back on his order; he will interrupt it and retract it, as it were, as if he were seized with regret, remorse, or repentance. For the God of Abraham, Isaac, and Jacob, as distinct from the God of philosophers and of ontotheology, is a God who retracts. But we should not be in too much of a hurry to give more contemporary names to the with-drawal of this retraction that precedes repentance, regret, and remorse.

According to this *third movement* from the beginning of *Fear and Trembling*, Abraham thus asks forgiveness for being prepared to make the worst sacrifice within the perspective of fulfilling his duty toward God. He asks God to forgive him for having consented to do what God himself had ordered him to do. Forgive me, my God,

---

draw Abraham into the equally paradoxical scene of forgiveness. Kierkegaard gives us at the same time the fiction and the truth, the true fiction that every scene of forgiveness perhaps continues to be.

for listening to you, is what he says in essence. That is a paradox that we shouldn't stop reflecting on. In particular it reveals a double secret law, a double constraint that is inherent in the vocation of forgiveness; something that never shows itself as such but always lets itself be understood: I don't ask you forgiveness for betraying, wounding, or doing harm to you, for lying to you or breaking an oath, I don't ask forgiveness for a misdeed, on the contrary I ask you to forgive me for listening to you, too faithfully, for too much fidelity to my sworn faith, for loving you, for preferring you, for choosing you and letting myself be chosen by you, for responding to you, for having said "here I am," and as a result, for having sacrificed the other to you, my other other, my other other in the person of my other absolute preference, my own, singular and plural, the best of what is mine, the best of my own ones, here Isaac. Isaac represents not only the one whom Abraham loved the most among his own, but also promise itself; he was the child of promise (18–21). It was that promise itself that he almost sacrificed, and that is again why he asks God for forgiveness, forgiveness for the worst: for consenting to put an end to the future to come, and hence to everything that gives breath to faith, to a faith or oath that is sworn, to the fidelity of every covenant. As though Abraham, speaking in his heart of hearts, were saying to God: forgive me for preferring the secret that binds me to you rather than the secret that binds me to the other other, to each and every other, for a secret love binds me to the one as to the other, and to mine.

This law reinscribes the unforgivable, and fault itself, within the heart of forgiveness requested or granted, as if one had always to be forgiven for forgiveness itself, on both sides of its address; and as if perjuring were always older and more resistant than what one had to be forgiven for as a fault, such as this or that broken oath [tel ou tel parjure], but which, by already ventriloquizing it, lends voice and gives movement to the fidelity of the oath that is sworn. Far from bringing it to an end, from dissolving or absolving it, forgiveness can then only extend the fault, it can only import into itself this self-contradiction, this unlivable dissidence within itself, and within the ipseity of the self itself, allowing it to survive in an interminable agony.

Here, then, is the *third movement*:

It was a quiet evening when Abraham rode out alone, and he rode to Mount Moriah; he threw himself down on his face, he prayed God to forgive him his sin [in other words, Abraham does not ask forgiveness of Isaac, but of God; somewhat in the way that the French Conference of Bishops didn't ask forgiveness of the Jews, but of God, even as they called upon the Jewish community to witness, in its own terms, the forgiveness asked of God. Here Abraham does not make Isaac a witness to the forgiveness that he, Abraham, asks of God for having wanted to put Isaac to death], that he had been willing to sacrifice Isaac, that the father had forgotten his duty to his son. He often rode his lonesome road, but he found no peace. He could not comprehend that it was a sin that he had been willing to sacrifice to God the best that he had, the possession for which he himself would have gladly died many times; and if it was a sin, if he had not loved Isaac in this manner, he could not understand that it could be forgiven, for what more terrible sin was there? (13)

In this fiction of a literary type, Abraham himself judges his sin to be unforgivable, and so he asks forgiveness. One never asks forgiveness except for the unforgivable. One never has to forgive the forgivable, such is the aporia of the im-possible pardon that we are meditating on here. Making his own judgment that his sin is unforgivable, which is a condition for asking forgiveness, Abraham does not know whether God has or will have forgiven him. In any case, forgiven or not, his sin will have remained what it was, unforgivable. That is why, in the end, God's response does not count as much as we might think; it does not affect Abraham's infinitely guilty conscience or abyssal repentance in its essence. Even if God grants him forgiveness in the present, even if we were to suppose still, in the past conditional, that he would have granted it to him, or in the future anterior, that he will have done so by staying his hand, by sending down an angel and allowing the substitution of a ram, it changes nothing in the unforgivable essence of the sin.

That is what Abraham himself feels within the nevertheless inaccessible secrecy of his heart of hearts. Whatever happens in respect of forgiveness, Abraham remains in secrecy, as does God, who in this movement neither appears nor speaks.

Even though my reading does not depend in the final analysis on Kierkegaard's interpretation, I will keep the latter in mind. What seems simply to require recall here is a type of absolute axiom. Which? Johannes de Silentio's determined insistence on Abraham's silence follows the highly original logic, aim, and writing of *Fear and Trembling: Dialectical Lyric*. Of course, for reasons that will become clearer later on, I am already alluding to the grand scene of the engagement to Regine and the relation to the father. As with *Repetition*, published the same year under the pseudonym of Constantin Constantius, there is in each case a sort of *Letter to His Father* before the event [*avant la lettre*]—before that by Kafka—signed by a son who publishes pseudonymously. My own insistence on the secret corresponds to a further decision with respect to reading that I intend to justify. Nevertheless, before all these decisions, a *factum* remains indisputable, and founds the absolute axiom. No one would dare dispute that the very brief narrative of what is called the sacrifice of Isaac or Isaac bound [*Is'hac aux liens* (Chouraqui)] leaves no doubt as to this *fact*: Abraham keeps silent, at least concerning the truth of what he is getting ready to do, as far as what he knows about it but also as far as what he doesn't know and finally will never know. Concerning God's precise, singular call and command, *Abraham says nothing and to no one*. Neither to Sarah, nor to his own, nor to humankind in general. He does not reveal his secret or divulge it in any familial or public, ethical, or political space. He does not expose it to any part of what Kierkegaard calls the generality. Kept to secrecy, kept in secret, kept by the secret that he keeps throughout this whole experience of asking forgiveness for the unforgivable that remains unforgivable, Abraham takes responsibility for a decision. But it is for a passive decision that consists in obeying, and for an obedience that is the very thing for which he has to be forgiven; and in the first place, if we follow Kierkegaard, to be forgiven by the very one whom he will have obeyed.

This is the responsible decision of a double secret doubly assigned. First secret: he must not reveal that God has called him and asked the greatest sacrifice of him in the tête-à-tête of an absolute covenant. This is the secret he knows and shares. Second secret, super-secret: the reason for or sense of the sacrificial demand. In this regard Abraham is held to secrecy quite simply because the secret remains secret to him. He is therefore held to secrecy not because he shares God's secret but because he doesn't share it. Although he is, in fact, as if passively held to the secret he doesn't know, any more than we do, he also takes passive *and* active responsibility, such as leads to a decision, for not asking God any questions, for not complaining, as Job did, of the worst that seems to threaten him at God's request. Now—and this is something that cannot be a simple interpretative hypothesis of mine—this request, this *test*, is consequently at least that of seeing just how far Abraham can go in keeping a secret, up to the point of the worst sacrifice, to the extreme testing point of the secret that is asked of him: that of death given, by his own hand, to what he loves most in the world, the putting to death of promise itself, of his love for the future and the future to come of his love.

TWO

Father, Son, and Literature

Let us leave Abraham there for the moment, and come back to that enigmatic prayer: "Pardon for not meaning (to say) . . . ," upon which a reader, one day, as if by chance, might stumble.

The reader looks for his bearings [*se cherche*]. He seeks his bearings by seeking to decipher a phrase which, fragmentary or not (both hypotheses are equally likely), could well be addressed to him also. For, at the point he finds himself, in suspended perplexity, he might, himself, have addressed this quasi-sentence to himself. In any case, it "herself" [*elle*] also addresses him, also addresses him as soon as and to the extent that he can read or hear it. He cannot exclude the possibility that this quasi-sentence, this specter of a phrase that he repeats and can now cite endlessly—"Pardon for not meaning (to say) . . ." —is a ploy [*feinte*], a fiction, even literature. Obviously this phrase refers. It is a reference. A French reader can understand its words and syntactical order. The movement of reference in it is undeniable or irreducible, but nothing would allow the origin and end of this prayer to be definitively determined, within the perspective of a full and assured judgment. We are told nothing concerning the identity of its signatory, addressee, and referent. The absence of a fully determinate context predisposes this phrase to secrecy and at the same time, conjointly, according to the conjunction that concerns us here, to its becoming-literary. Every text that is consigned to public space, that is relatively legible or intelligible, but whose content, sense, referent, signatory, and addressee are not fully determinable *realities*—realities that are at the same time *non-fictive* or *immune from all fiction*, realities that are delivered as such, by some intuition, to a determinate judgment—can become a *literary* object.

The reader therefore senses literature coming down the secret path of this secret, a secret that is at the same time kept and exposed, jealously sealed and open like a purloined letter. She has advance sense of [*pressent*] literature. She cannot exclude her own potential paralysis or hypnosis before these words. Perhaps she will never be able to respond *to* the question, nor even answer *for* this web of questions: who says what to whom in fact? who seems to be asking forgiveness for not . . . ? for not meaning (to say), but what? what does that mean? And indeed, why this "forgiveness"?

The investigator thus already sees himself in a situation that is no longer that of an interpreter, of an archeologist, of a hermeneut, in short, of a simple reader having the full status that such a one is acknowledged to have: exegete of sacred texts, detective, archivist, text-processor mechanic, etc. *Perhaps*, besides all that, he is already becoming a sort of literary critic, even a literary theorist, in any case a reader who is prey to literature, vulnerable to the question that torments every literary corpus and corporation. Not only "what is literature?" "what is the function of literature?" but "what relation can obtain between literature and sense? between literature and the undecidability of the secret?"

Everything is given over to the future of a "perhaps." For this little phrase seems to become literature by keeping more than one secret, and a secret which might, *perhaps, perhaps, not be one*, which might possess none of that hiddenness that *Fear and Trembling* was speaking of: the secret of what it signifies in general, and about which nothing is known, as well as the secret that it seems to admit to without revealing it, from the moment it says "Pardon for not meaning (to say) . . ." Pardon for keeping the secret, and the secret of a secret, the secret of an enigmatic "not meaning (to say)," of a not-meaning-to-say-such-and-such a secret, of a not-meaning-to-say-what-I-mean-to-say—or of not meaning at all, no way. A double secret, both public and private, manifest in its withdrawal, as phenomenal as it is nocturnal.

This is the secret *of* literature, the literature *and* secrecy to which a scene of forgiveness seems now to be added, in a still scarcely intelligible but probably not fortuitous manner. "Pardon for not meaning (to say)." But why "pardon?" Why should one ask forgiveness for "not meaning (to say) . . . ?"

The fabled reader, the reader of this fable for whom I am here playing the role of spokesman, asks himself if he is indeed reading what he reads. He seeks a sense for the fragment, which is perhaps not even a fragment or an aphorism. It is perhaps a whole sentence that wants to refrain from being sententious. This sentence, "Pardon for not meaning (to say)," simply stays up in the air. Even if it is written in the hardness of a stone, inscribed white on black on the board or confided black on white on an immobile paper surface, captured on the lighted screen (whose appearance, however, is airier or more liquid) of a gently purring computer, the sentence is still "up in the air." And being up in the air is what it keeps its secret of, the secret of a secret which is perhaps not one, and which, because of that fact, announces literature. Literature? At least that which, for several centuries, we have been calling literature, what is called literature, in Europe, but within a tradition that cannot not be inherited from the Bible, drawing its sense of forgiveness from it while at the same time asking forgiveness for betraying it. That is why I am here inscribing the question of secrecy as the secret of literature under the seemingly improbable sign of an Abrahamic origin. As though the essence of literature, in its strict sense, in the sense that this Western word retains in the West, were essentially descended from Abrahamic rather than Greek culture. As though it were living on the memory of this impossible forgiveness whose impossibility differs from one side to the other of the presumed frontier between Abrahamic and Greek culture. On one side and the other forgiveness is not known, if I may put it that way, it is known as *im-possible*, but—this is my hypothesis at least—the experience of this impossibility is received differently. Untranslatably different, no doubt, but the translation of that difference is what we shall perhaps attempt here, a little later.

The perhaps secretless secret of this phrase that remains up in the air, before or after a fall, according to the time of this potential fall, would be a sort of meteorite.

This phrase seems as phenomenal as a meteorite (the word is both male and female [*a deux sexes*] in French). Phenomenal is what the phrase appears to be, for in the first instance it *appears*. It appears, that is clear, it is even a hypothesis or certainty that goes without saying [*de principe*]. It manifests itself, it appears, but "up in the air," come from who knows where, in a seemingly contingent way. It is a contingent meteorite at the moment it touches ground (for the etymology of *contingency* also points to touching, tact, or contact), but without for all that insuring a pertinent reading (for the etymology of *pertinence* also points to touching, tact, or contact). Up in the air, it belongs to the air, to being-in-the-air. It has its dwelling place in the atmosphere we breathe, it dwells suspended in the air even when it touches. Even where it touches. That is why I call it *meteoric*. It keeps itself suspended, perhaps over a head, for example over Isaac's head at the moment Abraham raises his knife over him, when he knows no more than we do what is going to happen, why God has asked him in secret what he has asked of him, and why he is perhaps going to let him do or prevent him from doing what he has asked him to do without giving the least reason for it. Absolute secrecy, a secret to keep as a shared inheritance concerning a secret that can't be shared. Absolute dissymmetry.

There is another example that is very close to us, but is it another example? I am thinking of an unheard-of moment at the end of Kafka's *Letter to His Father*. This letter stands neither inside nor outside of literature. It *perhaps* derives from literature but is not contained within literature. In the last pages of this letter Kafka addresses to himself fictively, more fictively than ever, the letter that he thinks his father would have *wanted to*, would have *had to*, or *in any case would have been able to* address to him in response. "You could respond," "you could have responded" (*Du könntest . . . antworten*), the son says, which thus echoes like a complaint or countergrievance: you don't speak to me, in fact you have never responded to me and never will, you could respond, you could have, you should have responded. You have remained secret, a secret to me.

The father's fictive letter, included in the son's semifictive letter, compounds the grievances. The (fictive) father reproaches his son (who therefore reproaches *himself* for it) not only for his parasitism but *at the same time* for accusing him, the father, *both* for forgiving him *and* for thereby exculpating him. By writing to him, by writing to himself by means of the fictive pen of his father, Franz Kafka no more sees this spectral father than does Isaac see coming or understand Abraham, who in turn does not see God, neither seeing him coming nor seeing what he is getting at [*veut en venir*] at the moment of all these words.

What does this spectral father say to Franz Kafka, to this son who makes him speak like this, as a ventriloquist, at the end of his *Letter to His Father*, lending him his voice or allowing him to speak but at the same time dictating what he says, making him write a letter to his son in response to his own, as a sort of fiction within the fiction? (Play within a play, "the play's the thing." We are here spelling out the filiation of impossible filiations within this scene of secrecy, forgiveness, and literature: that of an Isaac whom his father was ready to kill; that of a Hamlet, who refuses to be called son by the king, his stepfather [*beau-père*], his mother's husband, his father-in-law,[1] father according to the law ["A little more than kin, and less than kind," he responds in an aside when the king calls him "my son" in act 1.2]; that of a Kierkegaard who had so much difficulty with the name and paternity of his father; finally that of Kafka, whose literature does little more, at bottom, than prosecute the trial *of* his father, both the case his father is prosecuting and the case against his father [*d'un génitif l'autre*]. Literature would begin wherever one no longer knows who writes and who signs the narrative of the call—and of the "Here I Am"—between the absolute Father and Son.

What then does the father say by means of the pen of the son, who remains master of the quotation marks? Let us select his arguments within an indictment whose dominant motif remains, for Kafka, *the impossibility of marriage*, motivated by a specular identification with the father, a projection based on identification that is at the

---

1. "Father-in-law" is in English in the original: *beau-père* means both "stepfather" and "father-in-law."—Trans.

same time inevitable and impossible. As with Abraham's family, as in *Hamlet*, as in what links *Repetition* to *Fear and Trembling* within the prospect of the impossible marriage to Regine, the basic question is that of marriage, more precisely the secret of "taking a wife." Getting married means doing and being like you, being strong, respectable, normal, etc. But as much as I have to do it, it is at the same time forbidden to me, I have to do it but I can't. Such is the folly of marriage, of what Kierkegaard would have called ethical normality:[2]

> Though marrying is the greatest thing of all and provides the most honorable independence, it also stands at the same time in the closest relation to you. To try to get out of this quandary has therefore a touch of madness about it, and every attempt is punished by being driven almost mad (*Hier hinauskommen zu wollen, hat deshalb etwas von Wahnsinn, und jeder Versuch wird fast damit gestraft*). . . . I must say that I would find such a mute, glum, dry, doomed son ("fallen," *verfallener Sohn*) unbearable; I daresay that, if there were no other possibility, I would flee from him, emigrate, as you had planned to do if I had married [we are already, always, within the specular address that is soon to become specular from the point of view of the father whom Franz is now going to pretend to allow to speak]. And this may also have had some influence on my incapacity

2. One could track this for a long time in Kierkegaard. I will note only this sign of it here: that the interpretation of Abraham's "incomprehensible" gesture—Kierkegaard insists on what is, for him, the necessary incomprehensibility of Abraham's behavior—works in particular through Abraham's silence, through the secret that is kept, even from those closest to him, in particular Sarah. That supposes a kind of marital rupture in this heteronomic instance, at the instant of obedience to the divine order and to the absolutely singular covenant with God. One cannot marry if one is to remain faithful to this God. One cannot marry before God. Yet the whole scene of the letter *to* the father, and especially the fictive letter *of* the father within it (literature within literature), is inscribed within a meditation on the impossibility of marriage, as though the secret of literature itself and of the literary vocation, were kept there: write *or* marry, that is the alternative, but also write in order not to go mad by getting married. Unless one were to marry so as not to go mad by writing. Mad about writing [*Fou d'écrire*, hence also "(one must be) mad to write."—Trans.].

to marry (*bei meiner Heiratsunfähigkeit*). . . . The most important obstacle to marriage, however, is the no longer eradicable conviction that what is essential to the support of a family and especially to its guidance, is what I have recognized in you; and indeed everything rolled into one, good and bad, as it is organically combined in you. . . . And now marry without going mad! (*Und jetzt heirate, ohne wahnsinnig zu werden!*) . . .

If you look at the reasons I offer for the fear I have of you, you might answer (*Du könnest . . . antworten*): . . . you too repudiate all guilt and responsibility (*Zuerst lehnst auch Du jede Schuld und Verantwortung von dir ab*); in this our methods are the same [Kafka thus has his father say that they both act by mirroring each other, doing the same thing]. But whereas I then attribute the sole guilt to you as frankly as I mean it, you want to be "overly clever" and "overly affectionate" (*"übergescheit" und "überzärtlich"*) at the same time and acquit me also of all guilt (*mich von jeder Schuld freisprechen*). Of course in the latter you only seem to succeed (and more you do not even want), and what appears between the lines, in spite of all the "turns of phrase" [your ways of speaking, your turns of phrase, your rhetoric, *Redensarten*] about character and nature and antagonism and helplessness, is that actually I have been the aggressor, while everything you were up to was self-defense. By now you would have achieved enough by your very insincerity (*Unaufrichtigkeit*), for you have proved three things (*Du hast dreierlei bewiesen*): first, that you are not guilty; second, that I am the guilty one; and third, that out of sheer magnanimity you are ready not only to forgive me (*bereit bist, nicht nur mir zu verzeihen*), but (what is both more and less) also to prove and be willing to believe yourself that—contrary to the truth—I am also not guilty.[3]

3. Franz Kafka, "Letter to His Father," in *The Sons*, trans. Ernst Kaiser and Eithne Wilkins, rev. Arthur S. Wensinger (New York: Schocken, 1989), 162–66.

Such an extraordinary speculation, such bottomless specularity. The son is speaking *to himself*. He speaks to himself in the name of his father. Taking his place and borrowing his voice, imputing certain words to him while at the same time ceding him the floor, he has his father say: you take me for the aggressor but I am innocent, you assume sovereignty by forgiving me, hence by asking yourself for forgiveness in my stead [*place*], then by granting me forgiveness and, by so doing, you score a double blow, the triple blow of accusing me, forgiving me, and exculpating me, so as to finish by believing me innocent at the very point where you had done all you could to accuse me, demanding as a surplus *my* innocence, which is yours since you identify with me. But this is what the father reminds him, in fact the law of the father that speaks through the mouth of the son speaking through the mouth of the father: if one cannot forgive without identifying with the guilty, neither can one forgive *and* render innocent at the same time. Forgiving means bestowing on the evil that one absolves the status of an unforgettable and unforgivable evil. By virtue of the same specular identification one cannot therefore exculpate by forgiving. One doesn't forgive someone who is innocent. If by forgiving one renders innocent, one is also guilty of forgiving. Forgiveness granted is as faulty as forgiveness requested; it admits the fault. Given that, one cannot forgive without being guilty and therefore without having to ask forgiveness for forgiving. "Forgive me for forgiving you" is a sentence that must be heard in every case of forgiveness, and in the first place because it guiltily assumes a certain sovereignty. But neither does it seem possible to silence the converse sentence: "Forgive me for asking forgiveness of you, which is to say in the first place for requiring you, by means of the identification that I am asking for, to bear my guilt, and the burden of the fault of having to forgive me." One of the causes of this aporia of forgiveness is the fact that one cannot forgive, ask, or grant forgiveness without this specular identification, without speaking in the other's stead and with the other's voice. Forgiving by means of this specular identification is not forgiving, because it doesn't mean forgiving the other *as such* for an evil *as such*.

We shall refrain from commenting on the end of this letter to the son, the fictive moment of an equally fictive *Letter to My Father*.

But it carries in its depths, perhaps, what is essential in this secret passage between secrecy and literature as an aporia of forgiveness. The accusation that the fictive father will never withdraw, the grievance that he never makes either symmetrical or specular (through the fictive voice of the son according to this legal fiction which, like paternity for Joyce, literature constitutes), is the accusation of parasitism. It runs throughout the letter, throughout the fiction and the fiction within the fiction. In the end it is literary writing itself that the father accuses of parasitism. Parasitism is the whole cause to which the son has devoted his life, everything to which he admits having unforgivably devoted his life. He has committed the error of writing instead of working; he has been content to write instead of marrying normally. In the name of the father, in the name of the father and of the son speaking *to himself* in the name of the father, in the name of the son denouncing himself in the name of the father, but without the holy spirit (unless Literature were to be playing at the Trinity here), everything here accuses parasitism and everything accuses itself of parasitism. The son is a parasite, as literature. For the accused, of whom it is now asked to ask for forgiveness, is literature. Literature is accused of parasitism and is begged to ask for forgiveness by owning up to this parasitism, by repenting of this sin of parasitism. That is true even of the fictive letter within the fictive letter. The latter therefore sees itself taken to court by the voice of the father inasmuch as that voice finds itself lent, borrowed, or parasited, written by the son: "If I am not very much mistaken," says the son-father, the father with the son's voice or the son with the father's voice, "you are preying on me [*vivre en parasite sur moi*] even with this letter itself (*Wenn ich nicht sehr irre, schmarotzest Du an mir auch noch mit diesem Brief als solchem*)" (167).

The father's indictment (spoken to the son through the voice of the son who speaks through the voice of the father) had previously developed this argument concerning parasitism and vampirism at some length. Distinguishing between chivalrous combat and that of the parasitic vermin (*den Kampf des Ungeziefers*) that sucks the blood of others, the father's voice is raised against a son who is not only "unfit for life" (*Lebensuntüchtig*) but also indifferent to this lack of fitness, insensitive to his heteronomic dependency, caring little for autonomy since he transfers responsibility (*Verantwortung*) for it to his father. "Be autonomous at least!" the intractable father seems to command. An example of this is the impossible marriage that is the subject of the letter: the son doesn't want to marry, but he accuses the father of forbidding him to marry "because of the 'disgrace' *(Schande)* this union would bring upon my name" (ibid.)—so says the father via the son's pen. It is therefore in the name of the name of the father—a name that is paralyzed, parasited, vampirized by what the son produces that almost amounts to literature—that this incredible scene gets written: as impossible scene of impossible forgiveness. Of and for an impossible marriage. But the secret of this letter, as we have suggested elsewhere concerning Paul Celan's "Todtnauberg,"[4] is that the impossible—impossible forgiveness, im-possible covenant or marriage—has perhaps taken place as this very letter, by means of the poetic madness of this event called *Letter to My Father*.

Literature will have been meteoric. Like secrecy. A meteor is called a *phenomenon*, such as appears in the brilliance or *phainesthai* of light, produced in the atmosphere. Like a type of rainbow. (I've never believed too much in what the rainbow is said to mean, but neither could I be insensitive, less than three days ago, to the rainbow that arched over the Tel Aviv airport as I was returning, first from Palestine, then again from Jerusalem, a few moments before—in an absolutely exceptional way, as never happens to such an extent—that city was buried under an almost diluvian snowfall, cutting it off from the rest of the world.) The meteorite's secret is that it becomes luminous upon, as one says, entering the earth's atmosphere, arriving from who knows where, but in any case from another body from which it has become detached. Then, what is meteoric must be brief, rapid, transitory. Furtive in its lightning passage, that is to say perhaps as clandestine and guilty as a thief. As brief as our still suspended phrase ("Pardon for not meaning [to say] . . ."). A question of time. At the outside of an instant.

---

4. See Jacques Derrida, "To Forgive: The Unforgivable and the Imprescriptible," trans. Elizabeth Rottenberg, in *Questioning God*, ed. John D. Caputo, Mark Dooley, and Michael J. Scanlon (Bloomington: Indiana University Press, 2001), 36–38.—Trans.

The life of a meteorite will have always been too short: the time of lightning, of a thunderclap, of a rainbow. Lightning, thunder, and the rainbow are defined as meteors. Rain also. It is easy to think of God, even the God of Abraham, speaking to us meteorically. He comes down upon us vertically, like rain, like a meteor. Unless it be that he descends by suspending his descent, by interrupting its movement. For example by saying to us "Pardon for not meaning (to say) . . ." Not that God himself says that, or retracts in that way, but that is perhaps what the "name of God" means to us.

A fabled reader finds himself represented here. He is at work. He thus seeks to decipher the sense of this phrase, the origin and destination of this message that carries nothing. This message is secret for the moment, but it does also say that a secret will be kept. And an infinite reader, the reader of infinity whom I see at work, is wondering whether this secret concerning secrecy is not *avowing* something like literature itself.

But why then speak here of avowals and forgiveness? Why would literature have to be avowed? avowed for what it doesn't show? Itself? Why forgiveness? Why would forgiveness, even a fictive forgiveness, be asked for here? For there is this word *pardon* in the meteorite "Pardon for not meaning (to say)." And what would forgiveness have to do with the double-bottomed secret of literature?

One would be wrong to think that forgiveness, presuming already that it functions vertically, is always requested from the bottom up, or is always granted top down. From most high down to earth. The fact that scenes of public repentance and pleas for forgiveness abound today, sometimes seeming to innovate in descending from the summits of the state, from the head or chief of state, sometimes also from the highest authorities of church, country, or nation state (France, Poland, Germany, not yet the Vatican), is not without precedent, even if in the past it was extremely rare. There was, for example, the act of repentance by the Emperor Theodosius the Great (ordered by Saint Ambrose).[5] More than once God

---

5. In *The City of God*, Augustine judged this act *mirabilius*. See Robert Dodaro, "Eloquent Lies, Just Wars, and the Politics of Persuasion: Reading Augustine's *City of God* in a 'Postmodern World.'" *Augustinian Studies* 25 (1994): 92–93.

himself seems to repent, to express regret or remorse. He seems to change his mind, to reproach himself for acting badly, to retract and undertake not to do it over again. And his gesture at least *resembles* a plea for forgiveness, a confession, an attempt at reconciliation. Restricting ourselves to this single example among others, didn't Yahweh go back on his error after the flood? Didn't he take it back? Didn't he repent, as though asking for forgiveness, in fact regretting the evil of a curse that he had pronounced, once he was faced with the sacrificial holocaust offered by Noah, and smelled the sweet and appeasing savor of the animal victims wafting up toward him; didn't he renounce the evil he had committed and the curse preceding that? Indeed, he writes,

> I will not again curse the ground any more for man's sake;
> for the imagination of man's heart *is* evil from his youth;
> neither will I again smite any more every thing living, as
> I have done.
>   While the earth remaineth, seedtime and harvest, and
> cold and heat, and summer and winter, and day and night
> shall not cease. (Genesis 8:21–22)

In the Chouraqui translation the word "curse" [*malédiction*], in its verb form *maudire*, is to be underlined even more, for it will shortly be contrasted with a blessing [*bénédiction*].[6] Follow God, see what he does, what he says. After confessing to a past curse, one he undertakes never to repeat, after having, in short, asked secretly for forgiveness, in his heart of hearts, as though he were speaking to himself, Jahweh is going to pronounce a benediction. The benediction will be a promise, hence the sworn pledge of a covenant. A covenant not with humans only, but with all animals, every living thing, a promise that we forget today every time that an animal is killed or maltreated. We should continue to meditate upon the

---

6. "Je n'ajouterai pas à maudire encore la glèbe à cause du glébeux [Adam]:
Oui, la formation du cœur du glébeux est un mal dès sa jeunesse.
Je n'ajouterai pas encore à frapper tout vivant, comme je l'ai fait.
Tous les jours de la terre encore, semence et moisson, froidure et chaleur, été et hiver, jour et nuit ne chômeront pas."

fact that the promise or pledge of this covenant took the form of a rainbow, which is to say of a meteorite, we should meditate on that while still following the traces of the secret, as well as what binds the experience of secrecy to that of the meteor.

God undertakes therefore to do no more what he has done. What he has done will have been the evil of a misdeed, an evil never to be repeated, and so having to be forgiven, even if by himself. But can one ever forgive oneself?

An immense question. For if God were to ask for forgiveness, of whom would he ask it? Who can forgive *him* for something, a misdeed (the question of "what")? or forgive *it*, itself (the question of "who"), the fact of having sinned? Who could forgive *him* or forgive *it*, if not himself? Can one ever ask oneself for forgiveness? But could one ever ask someone else for forgiveness, given—it seems, we are told—that I have to identify sufficiently with the other, with the victim, to ask him for forgiveness knowing of what I speak; knowing, in order to experience it in turn, *in place of him*, the evil that I have done to him? the evil that I continue to do to him, at the very moment of asking for forgiveness, that is to say at the moment of betraying him still, of prolonging the forswearing [*parjure*] that the pledge [*foi jurée*] will already have consisted of, its very infidelity? This question of the plea, this prayer for forgiveness to be given, seeks its undiscoverable location on the edge of literature, in the replacement of this "in the place of" that we recognized in the son's letter to his father as the father's letter to his son, from son to son as if from father to father.

Can one ask someone other than oneself for forgiveness? Can one ask one's self for forgiveness?

The two questions are equally impossible: they are the question *of* God (the question of "who"), of God's name, of what God's name means (the question of "what"), the question of forgiveness about which we have spoken, dividing as it does between the "who" and the "what." But dividing in such a way, also, as to discredit and ruin the distinction in advance, this impossible delineation of "who" and "what." Two questions to which one is always expected to respond *yes* and *no*, neither *yes* nor *no*.

THREE

More Than One

"Pardon for not meaning (to say) . . ."

Can that be forgiven?

For a French speaker who, short of any other context, wonders what to be forgiven (*se pardonner*) means, and whether it is possible, there reside in the expression *se pardonner* and in the ambiguity of its grammar two or three possibilities. First—but we consider such an eventuality to be a contingency—there would be this impersonal passivity of the turn of phrase "this fault is forgiven"[1] to signify "one forgives it," "it is forgiven," "it is forgivable." Let us look more closely at the other two possibilities, at the reciprocity between one and another and/or the reflexivity of self to self: "pardoning each other" and/or "pardoning oneself." A possibility and/or impossibility that is marked by two syntaxes, each of which remains, in its own way, identificatory and specular. It is a matter of what one might call, displacing the expression a little, a speculative grammar of forgiveness.

In terms of a trajectory toward a destination, how did Kafka's letter *from* his father inscribed within the letter *to* his father function?

---

1. *Pardonner* is intransitive in French, hence the passive "to be forgiven" can be conveyed only through the reflexive form *se pardonner*, and not by an ordinary passive as in English.—Trans.

the letter within Kafka's father's letter to his son (du *père de Kafka au fils*), who was signatory of the letter to Kafka's father (*au père de Kafka*), through all the genitives and all the signatures of this genealogy of forgiveness? Undeniably, the letter from father to son is also a letter from son to father and from son to son, a letter of one's own [*une lettre à soi*, also "to itself, to himself"] whose stakes remain those of forgiving the other by forgiving oneself. Fictive, literary, secret, but not necessarily private, the letter remains, without remaining, between the son and himself. But, sealed deep within the heart—in secrecy, or at least in the *secret*ary—of a son who writes to himself in order to exchange without exchanging this abyssal forgiveness with him who *is* his father (who in truth *becomes* his father and bears that name on the basis of this incredible scene of forgiveness), this secret letter becomes literature, in the literality of its letter(s), only once it exposes itself and risks becoming something public and publishable, an archive to be inherited, still a phenomenon, one of inheritance, or a will that Kafka doesn't destroy. For, as in the sacrifice of Isaac, which took place without witnesses, or whose only surviving witness was the son, namely a chosen beneficiary who saw his father's tortured visage at the moment he lifted the knife over him, it all comes down to us only in the trace left by an inheritance, a trace that remains legible but equally illegible. This trace left behind, this legacy, also represents, whether by design or by unconscious imprudence, the chance or risk of becoming a testamentary utterance within a literary corpus, becoming literary just by being left behind [*par cet abandon même*]. That abandonment is abandoned to its own drift by the undecidability—and hence by the secret—by the *destinerrance* of the origin and the end, of destination and addressee, of the sense and referent of the reference abiding as reference in its very suspension. All of that belongs to a literary corpus that is as undecidable as the signature of son and/or father, as undecidable as the voices and acts that are exchanged in it without exchanging anything (Kafka's "real" father, no more than Abraham, perhaps understood nothing, received nothing, heard nothing from his son; he perhaps was more asinine [*bête*] than all the said beasts, the ass and the ram who were perhaps the only ones thinking and seeing what was going on, what was happening to them, the only ones to know, in their bodies, who pays the price when men are forgiven, forgive each other, or forgive among themselves. I indeed said "men" and not "women," for the woman—about whom we shall see why and how she remains, like a wife, to be "taken"—clearly remains absent, spectacularly omitted from these scenes of forgiveness between father and son). A corpus as undecidable, therefore, as the exchange without exchange of a forgiveness that is named, requested, and granted as soon as it is named, a forgiveness so originary, a priori, and automatic, in short so narcissistic that one wonders whether it really took place, outside of literature. For the said "real" father knew nothing of it. Does a literary or fictive forgiveness amount to one? Unless it were the case that the most effective experience, the concrete endurance of a forgiveness either requested or granted, had—from the moment it became part and parcel of the postulation of secrecy—its destiny guaranteed in the cryptic gift of the poem, in the body of the literary crypt, as we were suggesting earlier in relation to "Todtnauberg," the scene of forgiveness between Heidegger and Celan. Forgiveness would thus be the poem, the gift of the poem. It doesn't have to be asked for. Contrary to what is often understood, in essence it must not be a response to a request.

In the "being forgiven" or "forgiving oneself" of the speculative grammar of *Letter to My Father*, we recognized a scene of forgiveness that was at the same time requested and granted, of and by oneself. That seems to be something that is both required and forbidden, inevitable and impossible, necessary and insignificant in the very test of forgiveness, in the essence or becoming-forgiveness of forgiveness. If there is a secret secret to forgiveness, it resides in its seeming to be destined at the same time to remain secret and to manifest itself (as secret), but also, by the same token, by means of specular identification, to become self-forgiveness, forgiveness of the self by itself, requested and granted by self to self in the ambiguity of *se pardonner*; but also canceled, deprived of sense by this very narcissistic reflexivity. Whence the risk of its sublated and sublating [*relevée et relevante*][2] nature, of the *Aufhebung* that we

2. Derrida has consistently rendered Hegel's *Aufhebung* by means of the verb *relever* ("to lift up," "raise," or "relieve"), but which also means "to add spice to."—Trans.

can get a taste of by citing another literary example that precisely seasons the code of speculative idealism with that of taste and cooking, namely *The Merchant of Venice* ("when mercy seasons [*relève*] justice"). One should ask forgiveness only of the other, the wholly other, the infinitely and irreducibly other other, and one should forgive only the infinitely other other—which is called "God" and at the same time excludes "God," the other name for forgiveness of oneself, for the *se-pardonner*.

As we have noted, after the flood comes God's retraction (let's not call it his repentance), this fallback movement by means of which God goes back on what he has done. In this way he doesn't just do an about-face vis-à-vis the evil done *to* man, that is to say, precisely, to a creature in whose heart malevolence dwells from the beginning and in such a way that God's abomination in the form of the flood will already have signified a sanction, a response, the retort of a punishment corresponding to the crime in the flesh of this creature, in the creature as flesh. Moreover, the evil in the heart of man must already have impelled the latter to expiation and pleas for forgiveness: an exchange of forgivenesses [*pardon contre pardon*] in the same way that one speaks of quid pro quo gifts. God's retraction, his promise not to do it again, to do nothing more evil, goes well beyond the human, which is the only species accused of malevolence. God retracts vis-à-vis *every thing living*. He retracts before himself, speaking to himself, but about every living thing and animality in general. And the covenant he is soon to make is a commitment with respect to every living thing.

We cannot become mired here in the immense (semantic and exegetical) question of God's retraction, of his going back on himself and on his creation, the question of all these movements of reflection and memory that lead him to go back over his shortcomings, as if he were at the same time finite and infinite (and we could also follow this tradition in Meister Eckhart, Jacob Boehme, Hegel, etc.). These cases of turning back on oneself should not be hastily translated as "regret," "remorse," or "repentance," even if the temptation to do so is strong and perhaps legitimate. Let us consider simply the doubling over, the retraction of a retraction, the sort of repentance of repentance that envelops, as it were, the covenant with Noah, his descendants, and the animals. Between two cases of God's going back on himself, between two retractions, the one that provokes the flood and the one that interrupts it, in the mean-time [*entre-temps*] of these two quasi-repentances on God's part, Noah is as if twice forgiven. On two occasions he finds grace. As though the Covenant between father and son could be sealed only through a repetition, a double coming-back, the coming back on oneself of this retreat or retraction, which, I insist, must not at this point be loaded with the attributes that a psychology, theology, or dogmatics to come will project upon regret, remorse, or repentance. Unless the latter notions were to depend, in their bottomless foundation, upon God's going back on himself, on this contract with the self by means of which God contracts to go back on himself in this way. The dissymmetrical contract of the Covenant seems thus to suppose the double trait of this retreat (*Entzug* in German), God's redoubled re-traction.

If the texts that we are going to read seem, therefore, to mean (to say) something—but do they want to say it? or are they asking us for forgiveness for not meaning (to say)?—it is perhaps something that should be heard even before any act of faith, before any accreditation granting them any status whatsoever: revealed word, myth, phantasmatic production, symptom, allegory of philosophical knowledge, poetic or literary fiction, etc. It is perhaps this minimal postulation, this nominal definition, which should then be connected with what we earlier called an "absolute axiom": a property of what is here called "God," "Jahweh," "Adonai," the tetragram, etc., consists in being able to retract, what others might call "to repent." This "God" has the attribute of being able to recall (himself), and to recall to himself that what he did was not necessarily well done, not perfect, not without fault or flaw. That would be the (hi)story of "God." On the other hand, even if one remains content to analyze the semantics of inherited words and concepts, namely inheritance itself, it is difficult to think a retraction that doesn't imply, at least in a virtual state, within the gesture of an avowal, a plea for forgiveness.

But asked by God of whom? Only two hypotheses are possible there, and they hold for every forgiveness: it can be asked either of the other or of oneself. The two possibilities remain irreducible, it is true, and yet they come down to the same thing. If I ask forgiveness of the other, of the victim of my fault, a victim therefore, necessarily, of some betrayal or broken oath, I am identifying myself with the other at least virtually, through the movement of retraction by which I affect, *auto-affect* or *hetero-affect*, myself. Forgiveness is thus always asked—by means of retraction—of oneself or of another, of another self. Here God would be asking virtual forgiveness of his creation, of his creature as of himself, for the fault he committed by creating humans who are evil in their hearts—which in the first place means, as we will hear, desiring humans, humans subject to sexual difference, men meant for woman, men moved by the desire to *take a woman* or wife. In any case, before one can detect in it any particular status and value, before one has to believe in it or not, this inherited text offers this reading: forgiveness is a history *of* God. It is written or addressed to the name of God. Forgiveness comes to pass as a covenant between God and God through the human. It comes to pass through the body of man, through the flaw that crosses through man [*à travers le travers de l'homme*], through man's evil or fault, which is nothing but his desire, and the place of the forgiveness *of* God, according to the genealogy, inheritance, and filiation of this double genitive. Saying that forgiveness is a history *of* God, an affair between God and God—and we humans are found from one end to the other of it—provides neither a reason for nor a means of dispensing with it. At least we have to realize that as soon as one says or hears "pardon"—and, for example, "pardon for not meaning (to say)"—well, God is mixed up in it. More precisely, the name of God has already been whispered. Conversely, as soon as one says "God" around us, someone is in the process of whispering "pardon." [Although reporting this anecdote is not essential to what I am developing here, I remember how one day on the sidelines of a dissertation defense Lévinas told me, with a sort of sad humor and ironic protestation: "Nowadays, when one says 'God,' one almost has to ask for forgiveness or excuse oneself: 'God,' if you'll pardon the expression . . ."

The first moment of divine retraction arrives when, as humans multiply on the surface of the earth, God sees their desire. It isn't said that God is jealous, but that he sees men desiring. His retraction begins when he sees man's desire, and sees that he is responsible for creating that desire. He sees that men perceive that "the daughters of men were fair." "And they took them wives of all which they chose" (Genesis 6:2). In Chouraqui's translation they took for themselves these daughters who were "fine [*bien*]."[3]

As always, desire is what engenders fault. It is (the) failing itself. It therefore governs the logic of repentance and forgiveness. Seeing that men were appropriating women for themselves, that they took wives (and, as in *Letter to My Father*, the scene of forgiveness, like that of betrayal and of broken oaths, turns around "taking a woman or wife"), God says (but to whom? he says it *to himself* therefore), "My spirit shall not always strive with man, for that he also *is* flesh: yet his days shall be an hundred and twenty years" (Genesis 6:3).[4]

Hence God "repents himself," as the Dhormes translation has it (noting also, in all seriousness, that "anthropomorphisms" abound in the narratives of chapters 2, 4, and 6); he "regrets" writes Chouraqui, to render a word that seems—or so they told me in Jerusalem—to mean something like "to console oneself." He goes in reverse in order to mourn, as it were, consoling himself. Apparently the verb has a relation of etymological resemblance with the proper name of Noah, as is often the case. But in spite of the small difference between "repent" and "regret," the two translations that I am citing are in agreement in saying, by means of the same expression, that Noah found "grace" in the eyes of Jahweh. Having regretted or repented for doing evil by creating such guileful [*malin*] humans, God in effect decides to exterminate the human race and to eliminate every trace of life on earth. He will thus extend the

3. "Et c'est quand le glébeux commence à se multiplier/sur les faces de la glèbe, des filles leur sont enfantées./Les fils des Elohîm voient les filles du glébeux: oui, elles sont bien./Ils se prennent des femmes parmi toutes celles qu'ils ont choisies." Cf. Dhormes: "Les filles des hommes étaient belles. Ils prirent donc pour eux des femmes parmi toutes celles qu'ils avaient élues."

4. Dhormes: "Mon esprit ne restera pas toujours dans l'homme, car il est encore chair. Ses jours seront de cent vingt ans." Chouraqui: "Mon souffle ne durera pas dans le glébeux en pérennité. Dans leur égarement, il est chair: ses jours sont de cent vingt ans."

genocidal annihilation to every living species, to all his creatures, with the gracious exception of Noah, his loved ones, and a couple from each animal species:

> And God saw that the wickedness of man was great in the earth, and that every imagination of the thoughts of his heart was only evil continually.
>
> And it *repented* the Lord that he had made man on the earth, and it grieved him at his heart.
>
> And the Lord said [but to whom is he now speaking? in secret or out loud? Is this not the origin of literature?], I will destroy man whom I have created from the face of the earth; both man and beast, and the creeping thing, and the fowls of the air; for it *repenteth* me that I have made them.
>
> But Noah found grace in the eyes of the Lord.
>
> These are the generations of Noah. (Genesis 6:5–9)

For our purposes here I shall simply recall, without reading it in its entirety, that Chouraqui's translation twice has "regret" rather than "repent," whereas it uses the same word "grace" for the fate that is reserved for Noah.

However one interprets the logic of this scene, one will hesitate forever between justice and perversion, as much in the act of reading as in what is given to read. We know the outcome of the grace that Noah finds in Jahweh's eyes, but does one have the right to translate it as "forgiveness?" Nothing, it seems to me, forbids that. God forgives Noah, him alone, along with his loved ones and a couple from each animal species. But in circumscribing his grace in such a terrible way, he punishes and destroys every other life on earth. Yet he proceeds to this very nearly absolute *pangenocide* in order to punish, and in a sudden feeling of regret for, an evil that, in short, he has himself committed: that of creating humans with evil in their hearts. As if he wouldn't forgive humans and the other living creatures for his own fault, the evil within them, namely their desire, whereas it was he who committed the sin of putting it in them. As if, in short, by the same token, he wouldn't forgive himself for the misdeed, the evil produced by his creation, namely man's desire.

If one is still wondering how and why, while regretting a misdeed [*méfait*], a bad-deed [*mal-fait*] over which he consoles himself badly, he allows himself to show mercy to or pardon [*gracier*] Noah and his loved ones, and to punish all other living things, let us now take into account two considerations relating to the sentence. In the first place Noah is said, immediately after this, to be a "just man." If therefore he is pardoned for being just, and God recognizes him as a just man, it is in the end because he is more just than God himself, not the God who recognizes him as just (one must be just for that), but the very God who has still to regret an evil from which he cannot exempt himself or for which he has difficulty forgiving himself. *As if*—I often say "as if" by design, as if I didn't mean (to say) what I am saying, and that would constitute the entry of revelation into literature—God were asking forgiveness of Noah or before Noah by making the pact or covenant with him immediately after that. In the second place, by also pardoning the pairs of animals taken into the Ark, by refraining from killing off the promise of life and regeneration, God doesn't pardon only Noah, his loved ones, and the couples from each species. By means of the justice shown to Noah he pardons by means of example a life to come, a life whose future or rebirth he wants to save. The Covenant works through this incredible grace, about which it is at bottom really difficult to know who grants it to whom, *in the name* of whom and of what.

Indeed, this punishment, grace, and covenant *in the name of whom and of what?* Apparently it is directed from God to Noah and his loved ones. But God punishes and pardons in order to forgive *himself* by *having himself* forgiven, in order to regret the evil and to pardon himself. And lo and behold the grace accorded to himself through the metonymy of Noah, in the name of God in the name of Noah, is extended exemplarily, even metonymically to all life, to all life to come, to all life to come back. Just before the Flood, after regretting the evil in his creation, God in fact says to Noah, "But with thee will I establish my covenant" (Genesis 6:18).[5] Noah the Just is then 600 years old. At the point of commanding

---

5. "J'établirai mon alliance avec toi" (Dhormes); "Je lève mon pacte avec toi " (Chouraqui).

him to board the ark God will say to him, "For thee have I seen righteous before me" (7:1).[6] The moment of the Covenant is thus situated within the great abyss of these forty days. Announced and promised at the beginning of the deluge, this moment is repeated and confirmed when, as Noah is arranging the "burnt-offerings" [*holocaustes* (Dhormes), *montées* (Chouraqui)] on the altar, God announces without regret, granted, but promising not to do it again, that he will no more curse the ground because of man, whose heart is evil, and that he will no more smite every living thing. By blessing Noah and his sons God confirms the covenant or the pact but also man's power over living things, over the animals of the earth. As though the covenant and abyssal forgiveness went hand in hand with man's sovereignty over the other living things. A *terrifying* sovereignty, whose terror is at the same time felt and imposed by the human, inflicted on the other living things. All that within the specularity of a God who has made man "in his own image," as his "replication" [*réplique* (Chouraqui)].

> And God blessed Noah and his sons, and said unto them, Be fruitful, and multiply, and replenish the earth.
>
> And the fear of you and the dread of you shall be upon every beast of the earth, and upon every fowl of the air, upon all that moveth upon the earth, and upon all the fishes of the sea; into your hand are they delivered.
>
> Every moving thing that liveth shall be meat for you; even as the green herb have I given you all things.
>
> But flesh with the life thereof, which is the blood thereof, shall ye not eat.
>
> And surely your blood of your lives will I require; at the hand of every beast will I require it, and at the hand of man; at the hand of every man's brother will I require the life of man.
>
> Whoso sheddeth man's blood, by man shall his blood be shed, for in the image of God made he man.

6. "J'ai vu que tu étais juste devant moi" (Dhormes); "Oui, j'ai vu, toi, un juste face à moi" (Chouraqui).

And you, be fruitful, and multiply; bring forth abundantly in the earth, and multiply therein. (Genesis 9:1–7)[7]

With his promise of a Covenant with man and all living things, God therefore undertakes not to start doing evil again. He will take steps so that "neither shall there any more be a flood to destroy the earth" (9:11). But in order to avoid this misdeed or infamy he will need an *aide-mémoire* or mnemonic, a sign in the world, a mnemotechnique that will no longer have the merely spontaneous form of a living and autoaffective memory. That sign will be the meteoric rainbow: "And the bow shall be in the cloud; and I will look upon it, that I may remember the everlasting covenant between God and every living creature of all flesh that is upon the earth" (9:16). "I will memorize my pact [*Je mémoriserai mon pacte*]" is Chouraqui's translation.

Immediately following that (Genesis 9:22), we are reminded that Ham saw his father's nakedness and reported it to his brothers. Is that a chance sequence of events? The fable that we never stop recounting, the ellipse of time of every (hi)story, is also the nudity of the father. When, after so many generations, the covenant is renewed with Abraham, it still occurs between two different times, before and after the supreme test. To begin, in a first time, God announces his covenant by commanding Abraham to be just and

7. Dhormes: "Elohîm bénit Noé et ses fils. Il leur dit: 'Fructifiez et multipliez-vous, remplissez la terre! La crainte et l'effroi que vous inspirerez s'imposeront à tous les animaux de la terre et à tous les oiseaux des cieux.'" [Chouraqui: "Votre frémissement, votre effarement seront sur tout vivant de la terre. (Your quivering, your trepidation, will be upon every living thing on the earth)." Dhormes, moreover, makes clear in a note that "the fear and dread that you will inspire (*la crainte et l'effroi que vous inspirerez*)" is literally "your fear and your dread." As if terror could be inspired only by first being felt and shared.] Tous ceux dont fourmille le sol et tous les poissons de la mer, il en sera livré à votre main. Tout ce qui remue et qui vit vous servira de nourriture, comme l'herbe verte: je vous ai donné tout cela. Seulement vous ne mangerez point la chair avec son âme, c'est-à-dire son sang. Pour ce qui est de votre sang, je le réclamerai, comme vos âmes: je le réclamerai de la main de tout animal, je réclamerai l'âme de l'homme de la main de l'homme, de la main d'un chacun l'âme de son frère. Qui répand le sang de l'homme, son sang par l'homme sera répandu, car à l'image d'Elohîm, Elohîm a fait l'homme. Quant à vous, fructifiez et multipliez-vous, foisonnez sur la terre et ayez autorité sur elle."

perfect (17:1–2), then, second time, after the said sacrifice of Isaac he confirms the same *by swearing* that he will bless him and multiply his seed (22:16–18). Let us pass in a single leap over all the cases of forgiveness and pardon such as the one Abraham asks for the righteous inhabitants of Sodom (18:22–33). Let us pass in a single leap over all the oaths, for example the covenant sworn with Abimelech at Beersheba, a covenant made in God's name (21:22–33), just before the trial involving the sacrifice of Isaac. Let us come back, all too rapidly, to what I began by calling the absolute axiom.

The axiom obliges us to pose or to suppose a demand for secrecy, a secret asked by God, by him who proposes or promises the covenant. Such a secret does not have the sense of something to hide as Kierkegaard seems to suggest. In the trial to which God submits Abraham, by means of the impossible command (for which one and the other have, in a way, to be forgiven), by means of the interruption of the sacrifice which resembles yet another pardon or a reward for keeping the secret, fidelity to the implicitly requested secret does not essentially relate to the content of something to hide (the command to make the sacrifice, etc.), but rather to the pure singularity of the face-to-face with God, the secret of this absolute relation. It is a secret without content, without any sense to be hidden, any secret other than the very request for secrecy, that is to say the absolute exclusivity of the relation between the one who calls and the one who responds "Here I am:" the condition of appeal and response, if there ever is such a thing, and presuming it can be conceived of in all purity. From that moment on there is nothing more sacred in the world for Abraham, for he is ready to sacrifice everything. This test would thus be a sort of absolute *desacralization* of the world. Besides, since there is no content to the secret itself, one cannot even say that the secret to be kept is sacred, that it is the only remaining sacredness. At the outside one could call it "holy [*saint*]" (in the sense of "separate"), but not sacred. (If literature, the modern thing that legitimately bears that name, "desacralizes" or "secularizes" the Scriptures, holy or sacred Scripture, it thereby repeats the sacrifice of Isaac, stripping it bare, delivering it and exposing it to the world.) As if God were to have said to Abraham, "Don't speak of it to anyone, not so that nobody *knows* (and in fact, it is not a question of *knowledge*), but so that there is no third party between us, nothing of what Kierkegaard will call the generality of the ethical, political, or juridical. Let there be no third party between us, no generality, no calculable knowledge, no conditional deliberation, no hypothesis, no hypothetical imperative, so that the covenant remains absolute and absolutely singular in its act of election. You will undertake not to open yourself up to anyone else. (Today we would say: 'You will not confide in anyone, you won't have confidence in any member of your family, you will open yourself neither to your loved ones, your relatives, or your friends, even if they are among the closest of the closest, you won't let your absolute confidants, your confessor, and especially not your psychoanalyst, suspect anything.') If you do, you will be betraying, breaking, and cheating on the absolute covenant that exists between us. And you are to be faithful, you must, at all costs, in the worst moment of the most extreme test, even if to do so means having to put to death what is dearest to you in the world, your son, that is to say in truth the future itself, the promise of a promise." In order for this request to have the sense of a trial, the veritable object of the divine injunction had to be something other than putting Isaac to death. Moreover, what interest could God have in the death of this child, even if it were offered as a sacrifice? That is something he will never have said or meant to say. The putting to death of Isaac therefore becomes secondary, which is an even more monstrous eventuality. In any case it is not the thing to be hidden, the content of a secret that is to be safeguarded. It has no sense. And everything will hang on this suspension of sense. God's injunction, his command, his request, his imperious prayer, are designed only to test Abraham's endurance, to put it to the test of an absolutely singular appeal. It is only a matter of his determination, his passive-and-active commitment not-to-be-able-to-mean-to-say, to keep a secret even under the worst conditions, hence unconditionally. To enter into an unconditionally singular covenant with God. Simply in order to *respond*, in a responsible way, to answer to the coresponsibility that is committed to by means of the appeal. That is the test of unconditionality in love, namely the oath sworn between two absolute singularities.

In order for that to be, nothing must be said and everything—at bottom, at the bottomless depths of this bottom—must mean (to say) nothing. "Pardon for not meaning (to say) . . ." In short, the secret to be kept would have, at bottom, to be without an object, without any object other than the unconditionally singular covenant, the mad love between God, Abraham, and what descends from him. His son and his name.

In the case of what descends from him, however, the singularity is sealed but necessarily betrayed by the inheritance that confirms, reads, and translates the covenant. By the testament itself.

What would literature have to do with the testamentary secret of this "pardon for not meaning (to say) . . . ," with the inheritance of this promise and this betrayal, with the forswearing that haunts this oath? What would literature have to do with a forgiveness [*pardon*] for the secret kept that could be a "pardon for not meaning (to say) . . . ?" In other words, in what way does literature descend from Abraham, in order to inherit from him at the same time as it betrays him? And in order to ask forgiveness for its broken oath? "Pardon for not meaning (to say) . . ." Is literature this forgiveness that is requested for the desacralization, what others would religiously call the secularization of a holy revelation? Forgiveness requested for the betrayal of the holy origin of forgiveness itself?

Whereas literature (in the strict sense, as modern Western institution) implies *in principle* the right to say everything and to hide everything, which makes it inseparable from a democracy to come;

whereas the presumed fictive structure of every work exonerates its signatory from responsibility, before political or civic law, for its sense and referent (what the *inside* of the text means and aims at, exhibits and encrypts, with the result that the text can always not *stop setting down* any sense or referent, not meaning [to say] anything), while at the same time increasing in inverse proportion, to infinity, responsibility for the singular event constituted by every work (a void and infinite responsibility, like that of Abraham);

whereas the secrets or effects of secrecy encrypted in such a literary event do not have to answer or correspond to any sense or reality in the world and appeal for a suspension of such (not for suspending reference, but for suspending, or placing within parentheses or quotation marks the *thesis* or arrest, the placing or stopping of determinate sense or real referent, whence the properly *phenomenological*, and therefore meteoric virtue of the *literary phenomenon*);

whereas literature is the place of all these secrets without secrecy, of all these crypts without depth, with no other basis than the abyss of the call or address, without any law other than the singularity of the event called *the work*;

whereas this literary right to fiction presumes a history that institutes an *authorization* (the status of an irresponsible *and* hyperresponsible *author*) of the performative decision to produce events which, to the extent that they are language acts, constitute so many addresses and responses;

whereas the coming about of this right implies an indissoluble covenant between an extreme autonomy (the democratic freedom of each and of all, etc.) and an extreme heteronomy (this right is given and may be withdrawn, being limited to the precarious frontier of the contract that demarcates literature on the basis of *external* criteria: no phrase is literary in itself nor does it reveal its "literariness" by means of an *internal* analysis; it becomes literary and acquires its literary *function* only according to context and convention, that is to say from nonliterary powers);

be it understood that literature surely inherits from a holy history within which the Abrahamic moment remains the essential secret (and who would deny that literature remains a religious remainder, a link to and relay for what is sacrosanct in a society without God?), while at the same time denying that history, appurtenance, and heritage. It denies that filiation. It betrays it in the double sense of the word: it is unfaithful to it, breaking with it at the very moment when it reveals its "truth" and uncovers its secret. Namely that of its own filiation: impossible possibility. This "truth" exists on the condition of a denial whose possibility was already implied by the binding of Isaac.

Literature can but ask forgiveness for this double betrayal. There is no literature that does not, from its very first word, ask for forgiveness. In the beginning was forgiveness. For nothing. For meaning (to say) nothing.

We shall stop here at the moment when God *swears*. Suspending the sacrifice by his own initiative, sending down his angel with a second address, he cries out, calls Abraham and *swears*. But he swears only *before himself*, saying it, avowing it, or claiming it. How could he do otherwise? Could he mean (to say) anything other than this tautology that means (to say) nothing?

At this instant, and on the basis of this instant alone, autonomy and heteronomy no longer add up to but One, yes, more than One [*ne font plus qu'Un, oui, plus qu'Un*].

> And the angel of the Lord called unto Abraham out of heaven the second time,
>
> And said, *By myself have I sworn*, saith the Lord, for because thou hast done this thing, and hast not withheld thy son, thine only son;
>
> That in blessing I will bless thee, and in multiplying I will multiply thy seed as the stars of the heaven and as the sand which is upon the sea shore; and thy seed shall possess the gate of his enemies. (Genesis 22:15–17, my emphasis)[8]

---

8. Dhormes: "L'Ange de Iahvé appela Abraham une deuxième fois du haut des cieux et dit: 'Par moi-même j'ai juré—oracle de Iahvé—que, puisque tu as fait cette chose et tu n'as pas refusé ton fils, ton unique, je te bénirai et je multiplierai ta race comme les étoiles des cieux et comme le sable qui est sur le rivage de la mer, si bien que ta race occupera la Porte de tes ennemis.'" Chouraqui: "Le messager de IhvH crie à Abrahâm/une deuxième fois des ciels./Il dit: 'Je le jure par moi, harangue de IhvH:/oui, puisque tu as fais cette parole/et que tu n'as pas épargné ton fils, ton unique,/oui, je te bénirai, je te bénirai,/je multiplierai ta semence,/comme les étoiles des ciels, comme le sable, sur la lèvre de la mer:/ta semence héritera la porte de ses ennemis.'"